JEWEL

JEWEL

RESTORING HIDDEN TREASURES THROUGH CHRIST

RANAE KAI BEAN

Copyright

Jewel Precious Jewel © 2021 by Ranae Kai Bean

Published by Ranae Kai Bean

ISBN 978-0-578-94099-1

PRINTED IN THE UNITED STATES OF AMERICA ISBN:

Holy Bible, New Living Translation, copyright © 1996, 2004, 2007, 2013, 2015 by Tyndale House Foundation. Used by permission of Tyndale House Publishers Inc., Carol Stream, Illinois 60188.

All rights reserved.

Scripture quotations from The Authorized (King James) Version. Rights in the Authorized Version in the United Kingdom are vested in the Crown. Reproduced by permission of the Crown's patentee, Cambridge University Press

Book Cover Design: Sophisticated Press LLC

DEDICATION

This book is dedicated to my sweet baby, my sweet angel, and my everlasting sweet sunshine whom I will cherish forever.

This book is dedicated to my near, future husband. I thank God for making us a great nation and creating us to be the perfect gift for each other on earth. I thank you for valuing my testimony and being bold to obey God's command.

This book is dedicated to every loving, beautiful soul. May this book encourage, strengthen, and purify your soul. You are precious, fearfully, and wonderfully made. You are the apple of God's eye. Repeat after me, "*I AM the apple of God's eye. I AM the apple of God's eye.*"

For thus says the Lord of hosts: "He sent Me after glory, to the nations which plunder you; for he who touches you touches the apple of His eye." Zechariah 2:8 NKJV

TABLE OF CONTENTS

Introduction *1*

1. Fall In Love With God 11
2. Fall In Love With Self 25
3. Protect Your Jewel 31
4. Nurture Your Jewel 45
5. Pray, Fast, Sow, Repeat 53
6. Focus 67
7. Mind, Body, Soul 87
8. Guard Your Heart, Protect Your Peace 109
9. Embrace Sexual Purity 121
10. Reflect 137
11. Rejuvenate 149
12. Trailblaze 163
13. "The Call" 179

Final thoughts *201*
References *203*
Notes *205*
About the Author *208*

INTRODUCTION

My name is Ranae Kai and I am from a very tiny island called Bermuda, located in the western North Atlantic Ocean, just a couple hundred miles from North Carolina, U.S. Call me biased, but Bermuda is breathtaking. Its natural beauty is unmatched, beaches are composed of soft, coral pink sand and rich turquoise ocean waves. While homes are proudly and joyfully represented in bright colors and white roof tops, piercing through our grand and proud palm trees. Best of all, Bermuda encompasses subtropical climates, hot and cool—best way to describe Bermuda if you ask me. Overall, I am grateful I get to call this very tiny island, *Home*. I get a first row seat to God's beautiful creation every day.

Just as the calm, soft, and coral pink sand, I too held a chill and gentle spirit. However, "in my day" I did not miss a *turn up*. By *turn up* I mean a party that included bumping, grinding, and very elicit romping. In other words, dancing within the imitations of "sex." I was basically moving along to music while performing very sexual positions. Culturally, this kind of dancing is intertwined with feel good reggae music, alcohol, and marijuana. And I was living for all the parties. Hence, I was usually the one who always initiated going out. It was as if I was secretly looking for something to completely satisfy me.

When moments of stillness would randomly hit me, those around me would always assume something was wrong with me. When really, my quietness was my way of processing or calculating. It's amazing how you can "know" people for years but truly not "know" them at all. I was the girl people thought they knew. But deep down, I made sure they didn't. I had to protect myself. Though I may have been out and about in the world, I was deeply longing for much more. That's when I began searching for true and pure freedom. In the search for such, I found a love unending from the most high, God.

I like to now consider myself, as a woman who has grown from being the wild extrovert to the coolest introvert with an extroverted type budget. I was once said to be the life of the party, and I enjoyed each moment until I didn't. Today, I am the life of my sacred place, my most recent apartment, where I shout for joy, praise the most high, and pray until the midnight hours. Originally, "happy hour" on a Friday night entailed drinking the night away while scouting my next sex partner for the night. Today, I spend my Friday nights in thanksgiving of God's grace and I wouldn't have it any other way.

Nevertheless, before I became the life of my own apartment, I was confined to a very small space where my Mother and I slept. Deep down, I wanted more from life. More opportunities, experiences, and beauty to embrace. I knew I needed to escape the life I was living and never look back. Though Bermuda was beautiful, I had too many painful memories of my life there. So, I decided I would start afresh in Mexico at seventeen years of age.

Through *The Rotary International Exchange* program, I made my dreams a reality. Unfortunately, the process was not smooth. Along the way, I was waitlisted and began praying without ceasing for God to come through for me. Secretly, I had a prayer life, but only when my life depended on it. Go figure! One morning, *The Rotary International Exchange* program called and gave me the best news ever! I remember jumping on my twin bed in absolute joy! I was happy and so honored to be awarded the opportunity to experience life in a new way. I yearned for "space" to think, create, and become. Finally, I was on my way.

Before you can savor this sweet moment with me, I have to tell you my truth. I have to share the journey that has brought me here, with you, in the pages of this book. You see, as a young girl, I didn't know the goodness of living for God. I just knew I had to be in control, I had to be strong, or else I'd get stuck. Before I knew it, I did get stuck. My control was actually my greatest weakness. And the enemy knew that. He lured me into living a life of sin because only then did I ever feel free from my reality. I escaped life through sex, drinking, and smoking. I was doing myself more harm than good, but numbing the pain was better.

* * *

For many years, I watched the spirit of "lack" lay on parents. That was frustrating. I knew I wanted something more for my life. Stability, space, and wealth became a longing desire. God knew my heart, but so did the enemy. Every move I made came with a distraction. As much as I wanted to be stable and free from my limiting lineage, the enemy did everything to derail me.

Growing up I heard, saw, and experienced some things a child only experiences in adulthood or never! Unfortunately, I was the exception. I remember watching my Daddy verbally and physically abuse my Mom. The hurt was great yet over and over again my heart ached. At a young age, I lost a school friend, Lynae. She was killed by her father. And as if that were not enough, my heart took another loss when my dear Pappa passed away. He was the only man I trusted and loved. How was I ever supposed to live without him?

With time, I became a pro at masking my emotions. No one seemed to care or understand how to support my needs or the needs of the children in the household. Though I was fed, clothed, and loved, I was lacking in emotional support. If only someone could initiate a conversation to speak of our hurt and fears, but no one did. Instead, we aimlessly allowed time to pass us by, hoping the hurt would go away. If anything, the pain grew. The adults knew just one phrase, "It will be okay. It's okay, they are in a better place." But that never healed any of our wounds.

As time passed by, I naturally developed who I was. Though not entirely wise, I was a fun girl to be with. I had a bold and fun personality. Believe it or not, at fourteen years of age, I had mastered the art of flirting. Flirting became another fun thing to do—which usually included a dirty response, a new phone number which eventually led to a one night stand, and ultimately a hard knock at life. Flirting was natural to me, completely effortless. That's when I discovered my "flirt maker." Basically, the boy who inspired my flirtatious ways had to be a smooth talker along with good looking, and that he was.

Eventually, I met my "flirt maker" but before we had any face to face interaction, we simply spoke on the phone continuously. This was right after Hurricane Florence in 2006. Following our phone conversations, we made it a point that we would eventually meet.

As we continued to speak our fondness of one another grew, as did our hormones. As I recall these memories, I remember the heartache I still felt from losing my friend and Pappa. Though I was flirting, my world was dark and cold. I was determined to make the most of life and meet the man of my dreams.

Finally, in 2007, I lost the little bit of innocence I had left. I sexted my boyfriend the entire night, anticipating our intimate affair. I was unbothered yet excited, I knew this would be a night to remember. As the rain began to fall, the mood began to set. At the eleventh hour of the night, I sneaked my boyfriend into my house and we embraced one another in my room.

I was happy and so excited to be with him, deep down I dreamt of forming a family of our own. I wanted nothing more than to create the life I had always longed for. After walking into my room and locking the door, we stood under the fan embracing each other. I was content. This moment could have lasted forever, but it didn't. Quickly, this beautiful and intimate moment turned into the question, "Are you ready?" Without hesitation I said yes, while asking if he had a condom.

I knew I wasn't his first, more like his fourth, but that didn't phase me then. If only I knew then what I know now. As he proceeded to coach me, he reassured me that I was in control. If at any moment I felt pain, he would pull back. In my mind, I was ready.

As he picked me up, I felt my innocence slip away. Nothing but our breaths could be heard. We intentionally remained cautiously silent as we were not the only people in the house. Go figure! Clearly, although I thought I was grown, I had no asset to my name. How or why I thought I could make such a grown decision at such a young age is beyond me. I was being played, played by the enemy.

That night, there was some blood and one tear—my innocence had officially been taken.

I am sharing this story because only in the last five years since that very moment of which I lost my innocence (ten years ago) have I learned how to overcome the schemes of the enemy and understood the importance of deliverance. You know the saying, "If only I knew then what I know now." Well, I am glad to say that today, I am led by God. Then, I was led by the devil. This book is for anyone needing wise counsel, just as I one day yearned it. Today, I want this book to be that for you. As I lay my life in the pages of this book, I do so with a humble heart. I hope my life can shed light on sex, purity, and the importance of Godly relationships.

Jewel is centered in protecting the gift God has given all women, our purity. God has allowed me to view purity as a precious Jewel. In this book, I will use the word *Jewel* to describe our purity and our most womanly and sacred of parts—our vagina. Before you begin to question this book, or the language in this book, I want to be completely transparent, helpful, and wise in what I say. For many decades, the world has derogatorily misused the word vagina—bringing shame unto women. Today, I want to break the stigma and use my testimony along with God's permission to refer to our hidden gem as a Jewel.

This book is designed to prophetically speak life and shed light onto the most sacred part of our body, the most private part. Other than our soul, heart, and mind which are indeed our most valuable parts, our Jewel is also very precious. Unfortunately, we have become severely unsensitized to having sex outside of marriage that we have forgotten God's desire for us. My testimony proves that God can help us regain authority over our bodies, even in the midst of pain, shame, and uncertainty.

Jewels are valuable. Jewels are precious. However, we haven't kept our Jewel private. The title of this book is designed to reshape the ill mindsets that have plagued our lives, ultimately influencing ill decisions. The word Jewel establishes power, honor, and respect when acknowledging the value of sex. Casual sex, fornication, masturbation, and adultery are deadly cycles that need to be stopped at its track. This book will help align our perspectives of sex to that of God's. Please also bear in mind that YOU are a perfectly designed Jewel. The goal is for you to also see yourself as God sees you.

As we begin to learn of our value in God, we will inevitably learn to respect our body. Afterall, we are beautifully and wonderfully made. I realized this as I conceived my first child. My sweet child was precious, a precious Jewel. My sweet child was an innocent precious Jewel that God created intricately in my womb.

At the tender age of twenty-three, I conceived a precious Jewel, which I no longer have the privilege and pleasure of knowing, meeting, or nurturing. The reality of an abortion was a decision I never imagined I would experience. The unknown was daunting. The unknown of who was my precious Jewel's father. The unknown of why I had been so ignorant over these past ten years. The unknown of where my life was drifting. My heart stopped, my life stopped at the thought of these unknowns, which was the result of pure ignorance because of the reckless choices that I had made. I prided myself in calculating moves. I prided myself in dodging bullets or so I thought.

Nevertheless, on March 20, 2014, as a part of me died, the life of my precious Jewel would forever be unknown. As I look up to the sky, half smiling, I know that I have an angel that will forever cover me; but the smile represents more than that. I also smile at the realization that this trauma has changed me for the better, yet I cannot overlook the trauma it took to change me.

I repent on behalf of every ignorant decision we make because of a quick fix, break, or temporary pleasure. Sex is not a quick fix. Sex is not a quick break. Sex is not a temporary pleasure. Now I know. We each have different stories and journeys. Let's learn from each other and create a community to uplift each other, to be better, and be purer. Let's pray and acknowledge God's perfection, creation, and authority.

Pray

Precious, Holy Father, who reigns over all the earth, we come before you with pure humility to seek your emotional peace, to seek your physical strength, and to seek your spiritual guidance. We come before you with surrendered and repented hearts to learn your perfect will of purity and celibacy. We come before you with praise and thanksgiving as we have the opportunity to be renewed, redeemed, revived, and restored. We come before you with pure love, joy, and peace oh Father. Oh Heavenly Father, our Great and merciful God, we adore you. May we love you more each day, may we fall more deeply in love with you oh Father. May we fall in love with all of your ways, words, and wonders. May we adorn you, may we be comforted by you, may we embrace and feel your tenderness. May we embrace all of you as you wrap your arms around us, guarding our mind, body, heart, soul, and spirit. May we have pure clarity in your Holiness, oh God! May we trust your perfect will, your perfect way, and surrender our entire beings mentally, physically, and emotionally to you and be nurtured spiritually by your Holy Word, Holy Spirit. May we embrace your healing oh heavenly Father, may we be comforted by your tenderness, trust your goodness, and surrender the very depth of our souls to you oh God.

We repent of our impure lifestyles.
We repent of fornicating, masturbating, lusting, and sexting.
We repent for impure hearts oh God, deceitful hearts oh God.
We repent for relying on our own strength and our own will.
We repent for choosing sin over choosing purity.

We command every familiar spirit of impatience, immorality, perversion, and abusiveness be cast out of our lives and burned with your Holy fire.
We bow before you to be delivered from evil oh God.

As you read on, you'll learn more about how my life soon reverted to darkness and how God's light has since become my fortress. My hope is that you too can find your way into God's unending love and grace to fully become who God has called you to be.

1

FALL IN LOVE WITH GOD

In my distress I called upon the LORD, And cried out to my God; He heard my voice from His temple, And my cry came before Him, even to His ears. **Psalm 18:6 NKJV**

The truth is God loves you deeply. He desires all of you, every single part of you. God only wishes for us to live justly and equitably. Even when we experience loss, hurt, pain, abuse, or trial, God wants to strengthen us through those moments, again justly and equitably. His love for you has never changed. His love is undeniable. He sincerely understands that life may seem unfair and burdensome. He sympathizes with our heartache because He first loved us, He is our first love.

From the very beginning, He created our inmost being, He formed us in our mother's womb, His love for us was instant (Ps. 139:13-14 NKJV). God has a sincere passion to fill us up with holiness, righteousness, and goodness so that we can walk in freedom and leave behind the shackles of immorality and torment. Thankfully, our love for God can be ignited through time, in the midst of pursuing a pure life. In order to do so, we must first repent and seek His Kingdom. Our flesh may be weak but *God* is our strength!

As we pursue the life God had originally intended for us, a life of unity, where we abide within God, Jesus, and the Holy Spirit, it is crucial that we come to terms with the condition of our soul. God understands that we have lost sensitivity to purity because of the intoxications of drugs, immorality, deceit, and the media. He knows our soul needs intensive nourishment from the heavenly realm and He is willing to give it freely so that we may begin to live fully. But before we can begin to reap the harvest set forth for us, we must begin to purposely detox from the world, only then will we be able to fall deeply in love with the purest of all loves, God's love. Start small. Talk to God. He yearns to hear from you. Don't hold back, He is for you. His love is unconditional and readily available for you.

Believe it or not, your words matter to God. Over and over again in scripture, we see the value in communication between God and His children. You are no different. God had a purpose for you, for your marriage, your family, your education, and business! God has no limits to what He can do; His purpose still lives. It's up to us to activate His will through our faith and obedience, or we'll miss our heavenly, supernatural blessing.

Nevertheless, our flaws and faults do not halt God's love for us. He has created you and me in His image! (Gen. 1:27). God's creation is perfect. Let that marinate for a bit. You are a precious and perfect Jewel. Zechariah 9:16 NKJV reminds us of this, "The Lord their God will save his people on that day as a shepherd saves his flock. They will sparkle in his land like jewels in a crown." You are that jewel! You have been perfectly designed to shine. It is up to you to own who you have been created to be and allow God to care for you.

So many stumbles in life have worn your shine out. God can polish you and restore all that you are, if you would just let Him. Colossians 2:5

NKJV reminds us, "Even though I'm separated from you geographically, my spirit is present there with you. And I'm overjoyed to see how disciplined and deeply committed you are because you have such a solid faith in Christ, the Anointed One." The Holy Spirit is seeking to revive and replenish our soul from all the gunk and grime it has accumulated through the years. Like a great polisher, God wants His light to shine right through our soul and reflect to whoever and whatever circumstances we may face. God is the greatest Polisher and Father. He wants the best for us. We are His jewels, His children. He longs to love and nurture our souls.

The same way God can restore our shine, God can fulfill the desires of our heart, more than our mother, father, significant other, or sex partner(s). Our pursuit for love has taken so many wrong turns before, leaving us lifeless, tarnished, and opaque. We've sought love in the wrong places. We've fallen victim to the flesh's impure nature while relying on sex to balance out our emptiness. But hear this, only God is equipped to instill the purity within us that has been lost. Though we may have grown distant to God and close to lust, fornication, masturbation, and sexting, God is always there to pick us up. Sexual immorality hurts you, but hurts God so much more. Let God restore your shine, let Him wipe away every tear and pain. Finally rest in His care.

In God's will you will find that, "God is our refuge and strength, a very present help in trouble" (Ps. 46:1 NKJV). Cry and seek His comfort. Cry and pour out your heart before Him. Cry. Cry Jewel, cry. Express your heartache and grief. Express your innermost pain. Scream or shout. He is your healer and affirmer. God is calling for you to let it all out, let it go. Only as we begin to open up our hearts to God are we able to feel faith rise. Through His power and glory, He transforms our minds, bodies, and souls. Our tears and our words are the catalyst to His power. When we surrender control, He is then able to do the full work within us.

Before we think, say or do, God already knows. But He desires that our will be aligned to His. When you finally communicate to God, He can begin to work. Sometimes you need only to talk to the Lord, share exactly how you feel. Release your thoughts unto God. Though He already knows your struggles and weaknesses, He appreciates when you acknowledge them as you pursue freedom and a genuine relationship with Him.

Prayer

Prayer is as simple as talking to a friend. God is always willing to listen, He is simply seeking your invitation to chat. Think of it like this, when you speak to your friend, you usually seek a place where interruptions are nonexistent, correct? Well then, do the same when speaking to God. Find a moment of stillness to pour out your heart. Whether you are sitting, bowing on your knees, or standing with your arms to your side or raised up to the Heavens, God sees your heart and how much you desire this moment. Rest assured, He knows your heart. Consequently, as you pray you'll want to also find stillness to hear from God. Hearing from God can be experienced in many ways, by enjoying His peace, instructing you to a specific passage in the Bible or He could pour out so much joy in you that you might wish to sing or praise dance! The options are limitless with God. Whatever it is, take hold of that moment, don't worry, He is there with you and for you. Savor the moment of peace, God is there with you.

Prayer is the key to wisdom and freedom in God, open up the door and experience all that God has for you. In everything you do, pray. As you wake, pray. As you prepare for the day, pray. As you get dressed, pray.

As you cook, pray. As you drive, pray. As you confront, pray. As you eat, pray. As you make decisions, pray. As you travel, pray. As you sleep, pray. Prayer is our spiritual hydration, with every sip we grow stronger and wiser. Remember, we must not live on bread alone, but by the very word of the Holy Bible (Matt. 4:4). God left us His word so that we may know the truth and run to Him in prayer when we need more understanding. Prayer is the glue that helps us stay aligned to God's plans, pray now and give God thanks for where you are right now. Whether good or bad, it is teaching you something. God will help you out and into a new season. Praise God for making you a precious jewel in His image, for this book, and for the many strategies ahead to fulfill your given purpose.

As you grow in your prayer life, make it fun! Take prayer walks, pray as you walk through the beach or a park, and express your desire to experience His presence. Build a prayer space in your home and be creative. Commit to corporate prayer, prayer walks andwrite daily entries in your journal dedicated to God. Whatever you choose, remember this time is special and unifying for you and the Father, the Son, and the Holy Spirit. Express your gratitude in this moment, confess your wrongs, and uplift others in prayer. Your prayers are ever so valued by God. When you pray, you acknowledge God's grace, power, and love. You are wholeheartedly worshipping in secret and *that* is very special to God. Continue praying and praising God. Watch as His faithfulness flourishes through your everydays.

As you continue praying, you will begin to desire more of God. More of His peace and love, which empowers you, inspires you, and helps you see life in a new way. Pay attention to the way God answers your prayers. Listen closely to His voice. Sometimes, He will use others around you to speak directly to you. For instance, a random person at the Farmer's Market may say, "Your presence is radiant." Or you may be on a prayer walk and look up to the sky and see the clouds and feel an immense sense of fulfillment and love, through those clouds you were able to read, "Love." Or maybe you're driving and you see a license plate that reads, "Joy." It's amazing how God acknowledges our prayers through natural signs, and of course His voice.

Don't cease in prayer, keep talking to God, pray for direction, pray that He continues to strengthen your faith. Don't grow weary, remain focused, persistent, and disciplined. Your prayers matter. God hears you. Don't give up now, the best is still ahead. Remember, God is our shield. He has overcome the world, with Him by our side, we too can overcome the sin that follows us. Our prayer is power. Take time to pray and let God in. Even to those dark places you purposely have locked away. God wants the good and the bad. It's the only way you will be able to experience complete freedom. Best of all, don't forget He loves you, unconditionally. You are his Jewel, His child, and He wants the very best for you.

Adoration

>...but the Lord your God turned the curse into a blessing for you, because the Lord your God loves you." (Deut. 23:5 NKJV)

>He is the Rock, His work is perfect; For all His ways are justice, A God of truth and without injustice; Righteous and upright is He." (Deut. 32:4 NKJV)

>In all your ways acknowledge Him, And He shall direct your paths." (Prv. 3:6 NKJV)

Once Upon A Time

At age twenty-eight, five years since making Jesus Lord of my life, I yearned for more. More than what church at the time was teaching. I needed to feel God's presence, hear God's voice, which led me to writing to you. I felt a void of uncertainty, and not entirely sure why or how I was in some situations. I was also experiencing doubt in a relationship, which I thought God wanted me to pursue. I then realized that I was not fully surrendered emotionally, when seeking clarity to end it or not. How did I realize this? Simple. I was unwilling to let it go. Instead of handing it over to God, I was persistent on managing the issue myself... so much for "Let go and Let God" right? Deep down, I knew God had better plans for me. But emotionally, I grew confused about this relationship. I questioned, how could this be?

After much tossing and turning, His voice led me to end the relationship. I thought I would marry this person one day, but God said, "I have more for you." And that was more than enough for me. How could I not trust God? Instead I dove into prayer. His voice and His presence gave me the peace that I needed to keep moving towards His Kingdom purpose. Although the decision to end the relationship brought along many tears, I knew everything would be ok with God by my side.

In all you do, be led by the Holy Spirit. Matthew 5:30 says, if your right hand causes you to sin, cut it off and throw it away. Seek His wisdom and it shall be given to you. Do not be lured into confusion or doubt, don't let the enemy have the upperhand. You are a child of God, seek your identity in Christ and watch how He restores your mind, heart, and soul. Don't stop praying, God is for you not against you.

Should you ever feel disconnected from God, pray! Look to his loving ways. Prayer has a way of bringing us back to our Heavenly Father. He is our safe haven, He cares for us, and His love is unconditional. Even when we are distracted by the world, He always finds a way to redirect our attention towards Him. All because He loves us and wants the best for us. There is nothing beyond God. Far beyond our flaws, He desires our attention to renew us and watch us carry out our God given purpose.

> Now the Lord descended in the cloud and stood with him there, and proclaimed the name of the Lord. And the Lord passed before him and proclaimed, "The Lord, the Lord God, merciful and gracious, longsuffering, and abounding in goodness and truth…" (Exod. 34: 5-6 NKJV)

God is our lifeline. When we adore God's magnificent ways, and we trust in Him alone, He equips us to conquer war, idolatry, backlash, retaliation, all the while strengthening our patience, love, joy, and peace. When we live a life of purpose and freedom within his love, that's when we show adoration for Him. In adoration towards God, we grow and are equipped to battle against any attacks from the enemy. Do not be tempted or swayed. God's fruitful spirits endure forever.

Temptation is real, we are flawed humans, but do not use your weakness as a crutch. Draw near and stay near to God in prayer. Prayer leads us to repentance which helps us deepen our faith and develop trust in God's promises (2 Cor. 7:10). Because of our sinful nature, relying on prayer to tackle our temptations is necessary (1 Cor. 10:13). The enemy even attempted to tempt our perfect example, Jesus Christ (Matt. 4:1-11). Flee from temptation, pray, and give God all you adoration.

Confessing

> But if we walk in the light as He is in the light, we have fellowship with one another, and the blood of Jesus Christ His Son cleanses us

from all sin. If we say that we have no sin, we deceive ourselves, and the truth is not in us. If we confess our sins, He is faithful and just to forgive us our sins and to cleanse us from all unrighteousness. (1 Jhn. 1:7-9 NKJV)

Fear not, for I am with you; be not dismayed, for I am your God; I will strengthen you, I will help you, I will uphold you with my righteous right hand. (Isa. 41:10 NKJV)

Yes, God is more than ready to overwhelm you with every form of grace, so that you will have more than enough of everything—every moment and in every way. He will make you overflow with abundance in every good thing you do. (2 Cor. 9:8 TPT)

It is crucial that we begin to confess who Jesus is and what He has done for us. In good times and in bad times, Jesus remains the same, He is the King of our salvation. We must confess the blood of the lamb in the name of Jesus. In confessing the blood of the lamb, we acknowledge our remorse for our shortcomings. We wholeheartedly seek His mercy and grace to further commit our lives to Him. Confession provides accountability and maturity as we decide to focus on the goodness of the Lord.

When we seek anything or anyone outside of God for fulfilment, rest assured we will always remain empty. It is essential that we take inventory of our lack so that we may see how our actions hinder our relationship with God. Perhaps we are seeking comfort, security, or excitement through sex. In hindsight, our distractions have caused us to lose our souls and grow more impure as the days go by. Being self aware of our thoughts, words, and actions is important if we intend to align our lives to God's standard.

Pouring out our dark lives before God is a process we need in order to heal ourselves and experience grace. Reflecting and learning from our mistakes before God will help to replenish wholeness. Confession is when we take personal ownership of our sin and seek to turn from it. We're deliberately seeking God's will. Just as we desire closeness to God, He too desires to unharden our hearts and undo all the noise that has caused division between us.

Guard your heart, remove the temptations to have idle sex. Confess and repent. Build your trust in God, rest assured, if Jesus was able to face severe temptation and retribution, you too can overcome. God is for us not against us, with Him we can do all things!

> He understands humanity, for as a Man, our magnificent King-Priest was tempted in every way just as we are, and conquered sin. (Heb. 4:15 TPT)

Thanksgiving

> God *is* my strength *and* power, And He makes my way perfect. (2 Sam. 22:33 NKJV)

Praying to God with a heart of gratitude brings glory to Him. Gratitude represents humility, forgiveness, and joy. Pure joy is a part of drawing nearer to God and growing in His spirit. Through Him, we are made new. Our salvation in Him is reason for great joy and thanksgiving. When we carry ourselves in thanksgiving, we give God liberty to free us and instill His love, power, and wisdom upon us. In effect, we begin to walk more confidently as children of God.

But let all who take refuge in you rejoice; let them ever sing for joy, and spread your protection over them, that those who love your name may exult in you. (Ps. 5:11 ESV)

Supplication

Be anxious for nothing, but in everything by prayer and supplication, with thanksgiving, let your requests be made known to God. (Phil. 4:6 NKJV)

Purity awaits the soul. Only God has the power, authority, and love to guide us through renewal. Praying with a fervent heart, as well as a soul of adoration, remorse, thanksgiving and supplication towards God will truly set us free. Requests of chains being broken, weapons being burned, and malice being abolished will bring us right with our Heavenly Father.

Repenting on behalf of others is also soothing and supports our healing journey. Praying for others' spiritual growth and emotional well being is a Godly level of maturity. We must pray without ceasing (1 Thes. 5:17). Commanding our rightful authority with Jesus Christ is a spiritual revelation as we recognize our powerful nature by God. God believes all we have is all we need as we faithfully seek Him.

Reflect

At this time, pause. Pray and repent. There is purpose in your life. Listen closely, let God speak to you and guide you in this gift called life.

Yes, God is more than ready to overwhelm you with every form of grace, so that you will have more than enough of everything—every moment and in every way. He will make you overflow with abundance in every good thing you do. (2 Cor. 9:8 TPT)

I am contending for you that your hearts will be wrapped in the comfort of heaven and woven together into love's fabric. This will give you access to all the riches of God as you experience the revelation of God's great mystery—Christ. For our spiritual wealth is in him, like hidden treasure waiting to be discovered—heaven's wisdom and endless riches of revelation knowledge. (Col. 2:2-3 TPT)

Even though I'm separated from you geographically, my spirit is present there with you. And I'm overjoyed to see how disciplined and deeply committed you are because you have such a solid faith in Christ, the Anointed One. (Col. 2:5 TPT)

Read 2 Corinthians 6 TPT
Read Psalm 143 NKJV

Repent

Express and disclose remorse of sin before God. Seek all of God. Pray without ceasing and acquire God's Holy language (1 Thes. 5:17). Strategize with God on how to overcome temptation. Rise above Satan's lies and triggers and begin to live fully in God's plan.

- What do you need to repent for? List every thought and action that has hurt God.
- How will you seek deliverance and healing?

Declare

- I am free of evil spirits, sickness, disease
- I am free of demonic spirits
- I am free of masturbation
- I am free of lying, stealing, and cheating
- I am free of aborted spirits, spirits of abortion preventing my growth
- The enemy will not prevail
- I am free of generational toxic relationships
- Lord deliver me from trauma
- Lord deliver me from child molestation
- Lord deliver me from perversion and homosexuality
- Lord deliver me from anger
- Lord deliver me from rejection
- Lord deliver me from abuse

In Jesus name, Amen.

2

FALL IN LOVE WITH SELF

For you are a holy people to the Lord your God; the Lord your God has chosen you to be a people for Himself, a special treasure above all the people on the face of the earth. **Deuteronomy 7:6 NKJV**

"...you *are* a chosen generation, a royal priesthood, a holy nation, His own special people, that you may proclaim the praises of Him who called you out of darkness into His marvelous light..." (1 Pet. 2:9 NKJV) Meditate on God's holy word and seek all the wonders of who you are in Him. Discover the beauty that you are, that you were created to be; all the beauty that makes you special and unique. You are treasured, you are gifted, says the Lord. You are a miracle, child, may you excel miraculously. May your precious, strong being have a sound mind and doctrine, yes, and amen! You are His shining armor, a part of His perfect creation. You are a precious Jewel. You are a precious Jewel. You are a precious Jewel. YOU ARE A PRECIOUS JEWEL! You are a sweet, perfect, precious Jewel.

Declare

I am a sweet precious Jewel, in the name of Jesus. Amen.

Your life is Special... Cherish It

Just as a Jewel, you are, "a precious stone, typically a single crystal or piece of a hard lustrous or translucent mineral cut into shape with flat facets or smoothed and polished for use as an ornament." (Lexico.com) We are God's chosen stones, firm and solid, yet delicate to the core. He built us to excel in all that we do. He built us to execute many fortunes. Only God truly knows everything about us and truly loves everything about us. Similarly to a Father who physically teaches and trains a child to take on the world, God is also there to teach us and be with us spiritually every single step of the way.

As we learn to love ourselves, God teaches us how to navigate our true purpose. God begins to direct our paths to communities, friendships, businesses, and lifestyles to embrace. When fueled and consumed by the goodness of God, He will naturally prepare our life partner. Before we know it, marriage could be closer than we can even imagine.

Let's pause here momentarily.

There are admirable, biblical characters like Paul, Jerermiah, Nehemiah, Martha, and John the Baptist who never married yet faithfully served the Lord with their life. Whether we are to be married or single until death, God's power and love will carry us in tremendous peace to fulfill our purpose. God desires for us to love every part of our being through Him, and thus He knows the desires of our heart and exactly what we need to fulfill our greatness. (Psalms 37:4 NKJV) With or without a supporting life partner, God knows what we need in every stage of our life.

It's important for us to learn to love who we have been created to be. When we love who we are, we inevitably fall in love with who God is and His creation. We are God's pride and joy. Afterall, we've been created in His image and have been blessed with strength, might, and heart. We are strong, mighty, and pure! Say this again, say it, write it, and believe it.

> You are the salt of the earth; but if the salt loses its flavor, how shall it be seasoned? It is then good for nothing thrown out and trampled underfoot by men." (Matt. 5:13 NKJV)

Something special and radical happens when we fall in love with ourselves. It's not a conceded type of love, but one of thanksgiving for being created in the image of God. Our self love becomes contagious. Our inner love and light attracts others to want the same. Because of this, let's rise! Rise to love and rise to peace.

With God we experience pure wholeness. We are royal, powerful beings in the Kingdom of God, called to walk with our heads held high. Why? Because we are loved by God. As we seek His will to overcome our spiritual, mental, emotional, and physical limitations, we become more Christlike. Day by day, we become exactly who we were created to be.

> Look to me and be saved… For I am God and there is no other." (Isa. 45:22 NKJV)

There is no one like you, no one. You have been uniquely formed. From your genetic makeup, to your smile, tone of voice, intelligence, train of thought, glow, and beautiful laugh. God values you, do you value yourself? Have you learned to cherish every part of who you are? Do you honor and respect your body as a special, precious Jewel? God does. He loves everything about you. He knitted you in your mother's womb and there is no mistake in you. You are perfect in God's eyes. God and you experienced the utmost quality time as He perfected you fearfully and wonderfully in the womb. May your soul truly know this very, very well. God was filled with pure joy as he designed your frame in His perfect image. You are a precious Jewel. You are more than a stone and crystal in God's eye, you are His child. God is in awe of your being, your presence, your love.

Whether you feel it or not, God is with you each and every day. God is omnipresent, omniscience, and omnipotence. His grace and strength are made perfect in your weakness (2 Cor. 12:9 NKJV). He will guide, protect, and shine favor upon you. He is for you. Our confidence, hope, and love are lovingly favored by our Most High God. Wherever you are, God is also (Gen. 28:15 NKJV).

Not only did God design you, He is still guiding you to your highest potential. He longs to hear from you, to speak to you, and fill you with confidence, hope, and love. Who we are is breathtaking. From the crown of our head to the soles of our feet we are perfectly made.

Jewel, precious Jewel, we are to love ourselves wholeheartedly just as God loves us. We are to love and be love; God is love. We are to experience love and embrace pure loving relationships. There is no room for imperfection, rather the understanding that we are perfectly imperfect. Failures are meant to be embraced. We are meant to make mistakes. Only then will we see God in action in our lives. Mistakes help us grow, just as rain helps a flower bloom.

In the meantime of your bloom, cherish this moment. Especially, if you are single or courting. Cherish your purity. Honor your purity onto God. Show yourself love by setting a standard of purity. Whether we have had sex, have sex, or have imagined having sex, we are missing the most precious moments that we can ever fathom as we welcome sexual purity. Welcoming sexual purity in our lives is a sweet pleasure. Although the world may market sex differently and devalue abstinence, remember God is pure and the world is impure. Abstinence enables us to grow on a level of oneness with God. Our focus is pure and our consciousness is clear. There is absolutely no means of distraction or dissatisfaction. Abstinence is joy for the brokenhearted. Abstinence is peace for the lost. Abstinence is freedom for the molested. Abstinence is love for the pained.

Abstinence allows for us to purely fall in love with self. Falling in love with self disinvites matters of the world that aim to temper our peace. Any form of ignorance, immaturity, or impurity must be kept far away. Consuming our mind, body, and soul with God is a Holy lifestyle for the fittest. Learning to say no to activities and involvements that do not serve us in growth is one of the greatest form of self love.

Reflect

Jewel, there's greatness inside of you. How have you or will, fuel your mind, body, and soul today?

Pray

All I have is all I need through Jesus Christ my Lord and Savior. I am free because of Christ Jesus. I am healed because of Christ Jesus. God's creation includes me and I will rise and glorify His Holy name in all that I do as I strive to purify my mind, body, soul, and spirit, daily.

Journal

For twenty minutes, write your response to this: I am a product of God.

Type *meditate* in the Blue Letter Bible phone application or website https://www.blueletterbible.org/ and write ten scriptures to reflect on.

3

PROTECT YOUR JEWEL

God's love is greater than lust or the desire to fornicate. God's love is the greatest love affair, it exudes a peace and joy greater than any sexual encounter. His love is unconditional, wonderful, and delightful. God designed sex to be a purposeful covenant between a Husband and a Wife. If your heart's desire is to be married, rest assured, God has the perfect life partner for you. But shall God not perceive the ministry of marriage on our behalf, may we too respect and trust God's will. Trust that God has your best in mine. Rely solely on His love, peace, and joy. God's ways are greater.

We have legal authority as children of God to decree the blood of the lamb over our life. Jesus interceded for us then and still will intercede for us today. Whether our transgressions are impure thoughts or sexual misconduct, God still hears our cry. We have hope and forgiveness in Him. Pray fervently, seek His wisdom, and you shall receive the peace and guidance that God desires for you.

Our legal authority to decree expands through various circumstances, for instance, we can command deliverance from our deeply rooted intoxications. These intoxications can be family traumas, ill family ties and or curses. That's right, you read that correctly, every person carries on generational strongholds. Thankfully, God is our deliverer, not man. With God, we can cast out whatever is holding us down. God will restore us and make us new.

> No temptation has overtaken you except such as is common to man; but God *is* faithful, who will not allow you to be tempted beyond what you are able, but with the temptation will also make the way of escape, that you may be able to bear *it*. (1 Cor. 10:13 NKJV)

We must seek God for strength and willpower to overcome our temptations. We must seek God's word for clear direction, comfort, and peace. God will help us protect our Jewel if we seek Him. Remember, your Jewel is sacred. Do not let sinful desires take away your peace. Granted, there will be many tests that will challenge our faith but which will also develop our character.

When we pray, when we grow, when we face temptation, we develop strength to overcome. But most importantly, we realize our worth and how important we are to the Kingdom of God. We are valuable Jewels, our Jewel is sacred and deserves the utmost protection. In order to protect, we must set boundaries. Boundaries with friends, places, and activities that no longer suit our needs. Our standard rises when we decide to walk in God's purpose. We begin to live on purpose for a purpose, anything and everything to stay in alignment with God.

Setting boundaries is life altering. Setting boundaries to protect your Jewel is even more so. Deciding not to have sex may seem hard and it will be, but it's worth it. Everyone is different, but some will have to purge their closet and rid themselves of certain clothing, others may have to stop listening to secular music or explicit television, and impure relationships.

You may even have to say goodbye to recreational substances like alcohol. Instead, secure meaningful time with God daily. Pick a place to speak to Him, read your Bible, Journal your thoughts and feelings to God, write any new learnings, pray, or simply be still in His presence. Sometimes, in the quietest of moments is when God begins to impart in us strategy. Strategy to flourish in this new journey. You are not alone in this journey, God is with you. Developing boundaries are made easy with our Father God who directs our paths as we acknowledge Him (Prv. 3:6 NKJV).

As you spend time in His presence, you will find that most of the Bible is about journeys, temptation, boundaries, and God's redemptive love. The Bible is the perfect companion during this time of renewing of our bodies, minds, and soul. It is important to note that our Jewels are not meant to be tried, cheated, abused, bruised, and scarred. Our Jewels are precious. Jewel, precious, Jewel, stop playing with death and start living the life God has designed perfectly for you. Only then will you find freedom and peace to be the real and wholesome Jewel.

Meditation

> This Book of the Law shall not depart from your mouth, but you shall meditate in it day and night, that you may observe to do according to all that is written in it. For then you will make your way prosperous, and then you will have good success. (Jos. 1:8 NKJV)

In order to protect your Jewel, you will have to meditate on the word of God, daily. He is our daily bread. With God by our side, the impossible will become possible. Without Him, we don't grow. Our minds require the Bible for strength and guidance. That does not mean we will not fail.

We are human, we will stumble, but remember God's word, "My grace is sufficient for you, for my power is made perfect in weakness" (2 Cor. 12:9 NKJV). We are stronger than our struggles, addictions, temptations, quarrels, and heartbreaks. We are greater than setbacks, pains, and illnesses. We are victorious. We are marvelous. We are a child of God, with Him all is possible.

Be a winner with God, He loves you deeply. Be a winner for God's Kingdom. Winning is God's way. Winning is the real good life. Winning is endearing the fullness of our life. With God, we rise joyfully because we are winners by Him. With God, we sing gladly because we are winning in His name. With God, we dance soulfully because we are winning His righteous race. With God, we love abundantly because God first loved us and we are winning on God's level.

Protecting your Jewel is the best self-love there is. Self-love is being a warrior not a worrier. As you learn to fully love yourself, find ways to discover your gifts and talents, find your Godfidence. The wisdom you acquire will leave no room for demonic tactics to deflect your journey and purpose. Look how far you've come and all the places you are going. Remain constant with God and watch how fear, discontentment, and ungodliness flee from you.

Acknowledgment and focus is the real sauce, the main ingredient, the necessary component in growing and blossoming. Acknowledge that you need a restart and your anchor is Jesus. Focus on God and learn the true value of self-love. For as you love yourself you will treat others, as others see how you love they will see God. Be the reason others come to God while you rejoice in your purity journey.

You are God's greatest and most beautiful creation, as is your brother and sister in Christ. Your journey aids those around you, whether you see it or not. Who you are, how you carry yourself, and what you do in secret hinders or aids the body of Christ. We are all a product of God's love, it is up to us to continue upholding that love and standard. You are a Jewel, you are valuable, hence by God's stripes we have been healed and reunited with the Father. Surrender your flaws, your pain, your control, and let God lead you. He is ever embracing and awaiting our surrender. It is solely up to YOU to invite God into your life-hence free will.

I am thankful that you have chosen out of your free will to read and learn from this book. *Jewel* is determined to share the many gems learned through virtual teachers like Tiphani Montgomery, Dominic and Lesley Osei. These phenomenal teachers excel in leading and serving. With this being said, Leslie Osei recently shared, "...hearers will always receive the fullness of God." Now, read that again. Dwell in that statement. When you seek God, you will find Him and He will make you whole. It is beneficial to learn from other brothers and sisters in Christ who have endured and who are mature in their faith. However, we should never substitute the Bible or our relationship with God with their experiences and life lessons. God speaks to every child uniquely, because everyone has a unique and special purpose. Living off of others faith or advice is a no, no. We may learn from mature leaders in the faith but we should always refer back to the word of God.

Just as God has come through for others, God will come through for you. God is our miracle worker. He makes a way out of no way. Whether our struggle is sex, drugs, self-esteem, depression, or finances...God will make a testimony out of your test! Someone else will also learn from your struggle and your victory. Rest in God's love, do not lose hope.

Just as you are a precious and valuable Jewel to God, so is His creation. Though we may look, think, dress, or speak differently, we are all similar in many ways. We breathe the same air, we share the same sun, moon, and stars and we are loved by the same God. A God who is great and grand. A God who protects and comforts. A God who loves unconditionally. Isn't it ironic that as much as we seek true love, our daily and hidden sin separates us from it? Thankfully, God is on a-whole-nother (*Bermuda accent*) level.

Once Upon A Time

In May 2015 I travelled to Israel!!! This place was never on my list of things to do. But God made it happen. He knew just how and where to meet me in this season. Israel was like no place I had ever been. I had no knowledge of God then, but I literally felt like I was in a sacred place filled with peace.

During that time, I attended a Cost Management class which just so happened to offer an immersive Global Marketing study in Israel! Honestly, I was very lost in terms of where my life was going but I was eager for more. Deep down, I knew nothing and no one would stop me.

Finally, once the day came and the fourteen hour flight was over, I couldn't get enough of Israel. Customer service was like no other, interactions were genuine, mannerisms were interesting, sentiments were one of a kind, overall everything and everyone was cool, calm, and collected. This place was spiritually magical. I learned so much about God, Jesus, and was dumbfounded that I was the only one that wasn't aware of all these stories. Nevertheless, though my classmates knew the stories, they had zero conviction. Whereas I knew nothing but was hooked! I mean, I walked the river where Jesus was baptized, gardens where so many of His teachings took place. God was speaking to me! I didn't even know He spoke!

Visiting Israel was life changing to say the least. I truly recommend it, especially if you are seeking a renewal of your mind, heart, and soul. Many people have overcomplicated God, when in reality He is so cool and always available. Whether we are in Israel, Bermuda, or any other country, God loves all of his Jewels. As we develop a relationship with God, we must intentionally seek to learn, love, and strategize daily to live according to His will. You are His Jewel, you are His masterpiece. Protect your Jewel at all costs, you are worth it.

Modesty

> Let the word of Christ live in you richly, flooding you with all wisdom. Apply the Scriptures as you teach and instruct one another with the Psalms, and with festive praises, and with prophetic songs given to you spontaneously by the Spirit, so sing to God with all your hearts! (Col. 3:16 TPT)

Serving God means we learn His word. Only then will we become filled with His wisdom. When we prioritize God in our daily life, we are able to minister to others by sharing revelations, testimonials, and stories that support them in their spiritual walk to Heaven. We include God in every decision we make. Our lifestyle should become one that is pleasing to God, walking the walk, talking the talk, and living the life He has ordained for us.

A lifestyle of purity comes with many learning curves, temptation is always lurking, but God always gives wisdom to overcome it. When temptation occurs, pray for wisdom and discernment. In my experience, God always provides wisdom to escape sexual situations and discernment to prevent sinful thirst. In one of God's discernment lessons, I felt very inclined to research the statistics for the average sexual partners in a person's lifetime. As I processed my thoughts, I heard God say, "Go, look it up. Provide some factual content to the amount of times we fail at securing a relationship or devalue our jewels." Sadly, laughter arose when

I read, "... these numbers are "ideal" for many in the U.S." The "ideal" number this article was referring to was seven partners for women and six partners for men. The big question is, when did more than one partner become ideal, let alone okay?

The fact is, that the "ideal" number is actually men and women in search of one true love, which we fail to secure without God. Some of us begin to have sex because of boredom, entertainment, or money, but really what we lack and long for is purity and security. Resuming to the statistics of average sex partners, there are various numbers throughout the years. Some statistics show two to four partners, while others average 7.2 partners. As of 2020, The United States and The United Kingdom showed seven to eight partners. While Homosexuals ranged from twelve to thirty. Prayerfully, the average lessens as hidden treasures are restored in Christ's name.

The ideal number for sexual partners in a lifetime should be one or none. We are too precious for the excessive sexting and sexual interactions. We are too valuable to be sleeping and fornicating casually, nonchalantly. God created us for more. Imagine the excessive soul ties taking place, what a mess! Clearly, we need more Jesus! The one who fills us with unending love. May we learn through this statistic the value of protecting our Jewel.

Our Jewels' purpose is purity. Our Jewels are not meant to be exposed to sex or sexing multiple people for the sake of securing the *right* partner. God has already taken care of the right relationship for us. He for one, is the perfect one and have a right and perfect fit for us. He will gladly reveal this confirmation with us. We must surrender our emotions to His glory and accept that our Jewel is precious and worthy of the wait.

Our Jewels are not meant to adapt to numerous different territories in a lifetime. We already have sufficient emotions and generational flaws to overcome. We are a whole lot on our own, and God is here to comfort us through. As we open up our sacred Jewels to Tom, Dick, Jerry, Sally, Sue, Jane, we expose our spirit of innocence. Yes, maybe sex appears as it's just "sex" after so many partners, however, that is very incorrect. Sex is deep and consists of intimacy and secrecy. Imagine the amount of hidden (known) and hidden (unknown) baggage we pour into others and vice versa. This is why we should remain pure and seek daily God's love and security.

Think of it this way, do not rush the process. Just as a mother nurses her newborn with breastmilk for them to grow strong and healthy, in the same way your purity serves purpose. In the meantime, get closer to God, read His word, pray, fast, discover your gifts and talents, but do not grow weary. Rest upon God, He is for you not against you.

As we read God's word and seek clarity through God's heavenly prayer language we gain revelation. We have to desire purpose to receive purpose. If we are not in search of a Godly purpose, there will be no result for confirmation. Remember, God desires all of us, we are His lost, sweet children. We are a part of His cherished creation. Until you learn and discover the importance of your purpose, you may continue diminishing the journey. For instance, if a small child throws a parent's iPhone in excitement to play, they may ruin it. While the parent may value the iPhone for communication, work, and memory creation, the child mistreats and undermines. Hence, the child must be taught what can be thrown for play versus what cannot. God teaches us the same.

God is always speaking, we must listen, hear, and obey. Let's not continue to fail because spiritual consequences are eternal. God cares for us, He desires for us to rejoice in heaven, which is the purpose of His parenting, and to prevent us from hell. Rather than experiencing a variation of hell on earth, we actually can embrace heaven on earth. Go figure, and it is beautifullll!

During my quiet time with God he whispered the following, "If you are so quick to try alcohol, drugs, and sex, fully aware of the damage and pain, you should be even more quick to try me." God is right. He has a splendid track record. He doesn't break his promises or leave us on 'read.' He tends to all of our needs, even the ones we don't even know we have. He desires that we surrender our entire being. We expose our souls in a manner in which God requires to be pure and intimate. God is crying His heart out that we repent and seek His guidance.

Unfortunately, we have become too confident in sin, and God wants us to become confident in Him. It's time to show our brokenness and stand in humility as He begins to heal every wound. The inner battles are too much to bear alone. God is waiting patiently to restore. Cry out to God. Though He knows your struggle, it is solely up to you to give God permission to heal you. It's been a long time coming, but it is time to die to self; allow God to renew you as you begin to live purely in your purpose.

> Baptism, which corresponds to this, now saves you, not as a removal of dirt from the body but as an appeal to God for a good conscience, through the resurrection of Jesus Christ… (1 Pet. 3:21 ESV)

Glorify

To glorify God is a lifetime commitment, one that we should forever cherish. Thankfully, our body serves as a way to show glory to God. Remaining pure or seeking purity in ourselves is a way to show reverence to God's desires. As children of God, we must seek and glorify God in all we do, say, and think. As we seek and find the glory of God, in Jesus name, we ought to respect His mighty throne, and repent faithfully.

Even as we glorify God, He is still at constant work. A very deep work within us. God's love never fails and is always the cure to each of our voids. You see, everyone is born with voids. As we entered an imperfect world ruled by sin (Genesis), we lost our pure and perfect nature. That is why a relationship with God is so crucial for our restoration and development.

Glorifying God means fighting the good fight to pursue more of His goodness with each decision. This good fight is the realest, most epic adventure we will ever endure. As tough and cold as the world may be because of destruction, God makes the experience all the better. Knowing that we conquer the odds is extreme boss moves. When the enemy aims to attack, God is there at our rescue. Imagine a street or school fight back in the day, you're about to get jumped! And you're waiting for your "crew" to rescue you… God is just that, the only crew we need. He always saves the day.

Fighting the good fight means we will fight temptation. Whether we're immersed in a sexual based conversation or we're in a public area immersed in sexual elicit music or television shows, without hesitation we must find an escape. We must guard our purity at all costs. Pray. Confess Bible verses over and over, listen to worship music on your headphones, and repeat! Protect your purity. Find strength in God when temptations occur.

Temptations are inevitable, but you are a child of God! You call the shots against ungodliness. As you continue to use God's word as a double edge sword, know you are protected and are fighting off the cycle trauma in your life. God's power is in you, afterall, you were created in His image! You are such a Jewel! Continue glorifying God in all you do, His grace will shower you with peace and strength for the journey ahead. Continue surrendering your body and will to God, allow His peace to overtake you. You deserve freedom from your past to accomplish your God given purpose. Remember, short term *fulfillment* of the world is simply expanding the void that can only be satisfied with the peace of our heavenly Father.

Strength

The greatest testimony of pure strength and power is Jesus. He conquered crucifixion. Though He physically suffered the most brutal death, being nailed to a cross, and bore the weight of hate, slander, and strife, He still surrendered His life for you and me. So that we may find strength in our heavenly Father. In layman's terms, Jesus *took the bullet for us*, so that we may have eternal life, pure freedom, and strength to lay down our lives daily for God.

> For what shall it profit a man, if he shall gain the whole world, and lose his own soul? (Mk 8:36 KJV)

God is our source of strength, love, and light. A gift freely given when we choose to die daily to our old, ungodly ways. When we completely surrender our life to God, He resurrects our souls. Until we surrender, we won't be able to experience the fullness of God's power and glory. Only with complete surrender can God purify our mind, body, and soul. Only then will we disengage in sexual immorality. Why? Because God's love is greater than our sexual desires.

Having sex without God's ordainment is selfish and insists that we choose our self over Him. This selfishness insists that we have no remorse for Jesus' death nor appreciate salvation. This selfishness insists that we rather "gain" the world and fulfill a temporary desire; meanwhile God has greater desires for our life. This selfishness insists that we rather lose our soul and be victim to our own demise, embrace the destruction of God's enemy; and God forever loves us, warning us in His holy word (Eph. 6: 10-11 NKJV). This selfishness insists that we prefer to submit to the devil and resists God's goodness (Jm. 4:7 NKJV). However, only the things we do for God truly matter in this life. When we choose God and put our selfish desires aside, He equips us for purity—protecting our Jewel. There is an abundance of wealth in knowledge when we choose God, it becomes a lifestyle of sweet adventures and endless revelations. It fills God with delight when He can work within us. In turn, we begin to learn and change our ways for the better to begin and continue the building of his Kingdom.

When we begin to work side by side with God, we see how important living a holy and pure life truly is. As we partner with God we are able to build ministries and sow into good ground. In other words, we are able to impact sons and daughters who like us need saving, restoration, and freedom. Through proper direction and time we will begin to reap powerful testimonies that have nothing to do with us, but everything to do with God. That my friend, is having faith with works and honoring obedience. As God leads and directs, we as faithful souls need to obey, execute, and build. In every season, even in our brokenness, we must remember all that God has done for us and everything He will continue to do when we embrace the Godly filled lifestyle.

4

NURTURE YOUR JEWEL

Abstaining from sex is not easy, with the absence of God. We regularly need to be reminded that the battle is actually not ours, rather the Lord's. The Lord humbly prides Himself in taking our battles. Why? Because we need not be indulging in them to begin with. Nurturing our Jewel is work equally, spiritually, emotionally, mentally, and physically, but enjoyable when it's honoring to God.

Commitment

How badly do you want to be set free? How far are you willing to go? Committing our mind, body, and spirit to living righteously for God is humbling and an adventure to say the least. Anything worth our time will require commitment and discipline. In this case, commitment to nurture our Jewel and discipliner will to make it a lifestyle. As we align ourselves with God's will, we'll find new strategies to abstain from sex, hence nurturing our Jewel while honoring God's plan for our life.

Nurturing our Jewel requires a mind shift: boldness, Godfidence, and security in who God has created us to be as well as His plans for our purity.

That focus will assist our commitment to nurture our Jewel. Remember, God is our standard and focus, we strive to live according to His will and glorify His name. As discussed previously, protect your environment, read God's word, pray, journal, and listen to music that leads you to Him, do not get distracted. Run your race, keep your eye on the prize, and watch how your commitment and obedience build unto the Kingdom of God.

> Enter by the narrow gate; for wide is the gate and broad is the way that leads to destruction, and there are many who go in by it. Because narrow is the gate and difficult is the way which leads to life, and there are few who find it. (Matt. 7:13-14 NKJV)

Godfidence

Being bold, confident, and secure is also a commendable cycle. God is pleased as we exemplify His qualities, shining amongst the crowd. Although the gate is narrow, why not choose life over death? Why not choose freedom over destruction? Why not choose peace over strife? Why not choose wholeness over brokenness? Why not choose purpose over pleasure? *Drops mic.* Afterall, life is better with God! You too can establish Godfidence.

As you work towards glorifying God, find time to build your Godfidence. How do you do that you ask? By forgiving yourself from your past mistakes and your current ones too. Let go of the bitterness holding you back from ultimate peace within. This is the greatest way to nurture your Jewel and your entire being. Life has left a lot of weight over us, God is here to remove that weight and give you freedom. Cry out to God, be sincere with Him, and ask Him to fill you. Walk proudly, you have a Father who loves you and who will always be there for you, no matter what. Let the peace of God take you high, His love is limitless. Hone in on your Godfidence, it's all yours.

Similar to forgiveness being more about self, less about others, our lifestyle change is of equal benefit. Change requires strength, resilience, persistence that only God can supply. God is supernatural, and as we pray and cover our lives with the blood of Jesus, in faith we receive. Without faith, receiving is in vain because we disregarded the supernatural power of God. Be bold in your faith, know that God will supply your needs. Leave no room for doubt. He has brought you this far, won't He take you further? Discover your Godfidence, learn His word, declutter your mind, and watch as you become an unstoppable force as you dive into His promises.

Confront

Have you found that what usually glitters is not gold? Many times we hold onto what glitters because it looks good or feels good, but adds zero value to our purpose. Montgomery shared a live video stating, "When we are not required to change we gladly cling to what "feels" good" (2020). This could not be more true. Complacency is our biggest giant, one we must defeat daily with the word of God and our deliberate actions for change.

Life will always provide counterfeit solutions that are easy and feel good, but as long as you KNOW there is only one God who has overcome, you will rest easy knowing He is in control. There is no need for you to look elsewhere when God is right here. With God and lots of faith, your temptations and obstacles will dissipate. Instead, focus on getting to the root of your problem. Give God full control to examine those areas and let him clean, repair, love, and heal the root of your pain.

You are deserving of care. For far too long you have avoided the truth of your pain. When we are sincere with ourselves and allow God to step in, we realize all we had to do was confront the issue head on...I understand the avoidance, it hurts to relive the truth of our past. But you can move forward without the pain, it's only a matter of changing the way we think. I'll say it again, YOU are deserving of care, of a fresh start, and of a pain free future. Confront what is bothering you, what has caused you to stumble, and what you keep going back to. Strategize with God ways to do better and do it. Forgive yourself of the past and move forward. You are a Jewel, created for greatness, it's time to move forward in excellence.

Precious Jewel

Precious Jewel, as a jewel is prepared for jewelry, we are prepared for purity. The correlation between a jewels refinement aligns completely with our process. We too are in a journey to perfect every bit of who we are, in accordance to God's design. Unfortunately, because we were born with a void our relationship with God and purity was affected. Adam and Eve's disobedience caused a separation between creation and our heavenly Father, but thankfully, Jesus redeemed it for us. The enemy tried it! But Jesus had the last word. We have since been restored into the Jewel we were created to be, by His great grace.

A little backstory on the creation of jewels, gemstones are mineral based with the potential to shine, making it a desirable selling point. Once the gemstones are cut and polished they are used for jewelry. The final form of a jewel has experienced an extended level of work, usually increasing its value. Similarly, our sinful nature needs to be cut and our soul needs to be polished. We too are hidden gems in need of nurturing and refinement for a greater purpose, shall we choose to give God control of our process. He has created us uniquely and at the right time, we too will shine bright. Our shine will guide others in their journeys. Our shine is worth the process.

God delights in making us clean and new. Just take a look at the book of Zachariah chapter nine. The book begins with a cry and a call to the Lord, for His children to turn from their sinful and evil ways. By the grace of God, His children were humbled and reverted to a clean heart and were made new. Through this testament, we learn that it is not by His power nor by His might, but by His spirit that we are made well, whole and pure (Zec. 4:6 NKJV). God's spirit is our refinement. God promises us that as He began a good work within us, He too will bring it to fruition as we proclaim His Holy name (Phil. 1:6 NKJV). In order to discover our pure gifts and talents there is a process of refinement required. We must trust and believe that we in fact are precious, valuable jewels, with purpose.

In fulfilling our purpose, God requires us to undergo character and heart checks. God gladly plants and waters our valuable seeds of righteousness, while He uproots our seeds of unrighteousness. He also faithfully reminds us that our true value is in Christ, and therefore a spiritual refinement is required to enhance our value. This process is similar to resurrection, allowing us to be the best version of ourselves, of the greatest value. Christ actually being the best version, with the greatest value, created for us to learn from. Hence, nurturing our gifts allows them to be nourished and reestablished in value. Nurturing our Jewels requires us to value them. In nurturing our Jewels, we gain an understanding of our creator's principles and standards. Our Jewels are worthy and we are worthy. May we value the significance of our Jewels and live to value the importance of sex. Only when we establish the value of our Jewel can we nurture with respect, dignity, and discipline

May we repent of our selfish desires, and recognize the dangers when we abuse our jewels and abuse His mercy. May repentance become a part of our daily lifestyle, a daily form of humility as we come before God. As we seek purity wholeheartedly, may we desire more of God's way and less of our way? And may we take heed to the prestige queens and kings God created us to be. May God's favor and grace be upon us all as we go through refinement.

Precious Jewel, the process takes time but when times are weary, pray. Prayer is our communication with God and our armour for battle. Thank God for his peace, love, and joy. Praise God for healing and deliverance. Admire God for His power and greatness. Acknowledge God for rescuing and saving us. And repent wholeheartedly, accept God's love and live purely.

Intimacy

Our Jewels were created for intimacy with one special partner, for one special purpose. The purpose in the one special partner is to multiply, while to not deprive our spouse from sex (1 Cor. 7:5 NKJV). Given God's unconditional love, His will requires our sincere obedience. Nothing is impossible with God, which clearly is all the reason to prioritize our relationship with Him. We must become diligent in prayer and with regards to marriage place a demand on our offerings unto God shall the desire to marry be gifted unto us. Proactively covering our spouse in prayer exercising wisdom. Understanding God's word and how to pray is essential throughout our journey; may we live to grow deeper in His goodness. May we learn to nurture our Jewels in this season.

The Bible is a sweet love story full of the most explicit life lessons. Overall, we learn that God has created us for more than a *quick fix*, *summer fling, friend with benefit,* or *one night stand.* He created us for more than drama, altercation, chaos, and arguments. The battle against all we know is real. We must put the proper armour on to fight and face where we need fixing. Thankfully, with God nothing is impossible, even if it may seem it. Protecting our Jewel means we honor God's command by nurturing our Jewel, living pure, praying, and fasting. This way of life has to become second nature. Do not grow weary, when we are weak, God makes us strong. His mercy endures forever. Nurture your Jewel.

> Concerning this thing I pleaded with the Lord three times that it might depart from me. And He said to me, "My grace is sufficient for you, for My strength is made perfect in weakness." Therefore most gladly I will rather boast in my infirmities, that the power of Christ may rest upon me. Therefore I take pleasure in infirmities, in reproaches, in needs, in persecutions, in distresses, for Christ's sake. For when I am weak, then I am strong. (2 Cor. 12:9-10 NKJV)

5

PRAY, FAST, SOW, REPEAT

And we have known and believed the love that God has for us. God is love, and he who abides in love abides in God, and God in him.
1 John 4:16 NKJV

We are children of God. Purification is essential in establishing lifelong peace with God, our heavenly Father. Prayer and reverence is a must. Pray and ask God to help you understand the importance of purity. Understanding the importance of purity allows us to truly value our covenant with God. Picture this: A beautiful and prominent tree planted by the stream of a river, but just as it begins to flourish, it faces disaster. A hurricane begins to damage its beauty and purpose. Now imagine the same scenario but regarding your purity—you are the tree.

Sexual activity before marriage hinders your Jewel. Just like this beautiful yet innocent tree, we were born ready to bloom, develop, and become equipped for our intended purpose. However our sin and immorality cause a detour in our progress. We become our greatest battle to overturn.

Now, let's be clear, there is no excuse for having sex outside of marriage. Dating/courting is also not an excuse to do what only married people should be doing. We must set expectations and standards in all relationships. Blurred lines are not acceptable. A sound foundation needs to be set. Our purity must be respected, but before it's respected by others, it must be respected by the Jewel holder. Therefore, I encourage and stand behind the act of abstinence.

> And whatever we ask we receive from Him, because we keep His commandments and do those things that are pleasing in His sight. (1 Jn. 3:22 NKJV)

God is perfect. And though we are imperfectly perfect, we were made in perfect love. Like Jesus, we were made in the image of God. Just as Christ loved the world, we too must find our Godfidence and learn to love ourselves as we would love others.

> Beloved, let us love one another, for love is of God; and everyone who loves is born of God and knows God… In this the love of God was manifested toward us, that God has sent His only begotten Son into the world, that we might live through Him. (1 Jn. 4:7,9 NKJV)

Prayer & Fasting

Praying to God helps us to walk according to His will. Something special happens when we as a child seek the voice of our heavenly Father, God seems to just melt for our love. That's how much He loves us. He yearns to hear from us and we should too. Having a direct conversation with God helps us better understand who He is and who we are. Our purpose is more attainable when we first seek God through prayer.

Prayer is a fun and therapeutic way to communicate with God. As we share our heart a sweet rapport begins to build. Trust is the foundation of all relationships and one of God's biggest interests. Building this trust factor allows us to be the most transparent and open. God wants just that, our tears, frustrations, misunderstandings, and ultimately our heart. Prayer releases the walls developed around our heart over time and soothes our soul. Committing to prayer walks, creating a prayer journal, securing a prayer partner, and reading through Psalms are beautiful ways to experience the presence of God.

Your Jewel is special. Your Jewel is luxury. Your Jewel is priceless. Just as there is only one you, there is only one Jewel that was created within you. Your Jewel is sacred. There need not be multiple keys unlocking our sacred treasure. There need not be any regular door knocks. Our heavenly father who reigns supreme over all the earth, knows our every desire and has already, especially secured the time and place that we will encounter our significant other. And this is His will. God values marriages. He too knows what's best for us. For some it's marriage for others it's an eternal marriage with God. Either way, pray. Submit your heart to God.

Praying and fasting prepares us for supernatural encounters. Prayer and fasting is an opportunity to faithfully, wholeheartedly seek and rely on our heavenly father. God provides comfort and peace as we bow before Him seeking His face. Prayer is fulfilling and uplifting. As we draw near to Him, our desires will align with His. Although we may have many thoughts about what we envisioned our life to be, God has ordained a better way.

Developing sensitivity to His voice and Holy Spirit through prayer is the absolute best direction we will ever have to conquer life. Fasting does just that. Fasting is the complete reliance on God as you rely on His spiritual strength, than the physical strength of food. God honors obedience and values sacrifice. Exercising and lifting weight expands our physical muscles while fasting develops our spiritual muscle. God is there with you. He loves your dedication and finds joy in your process.

As we pray we must seek to be more like God and less like us. Unfortunately, we will have to unlearn many characteristics and practices, yet fortunately we have grace to be made new. Never forget that especially in our weakness, God's power is strengthened. He is your fortress and your covering. Whatever the circumstance, pray. If needed, try walks devoted to prayer. As you walk, fill your heart with thanksgiving. Acknowledge God for the gift of life and the beauty all around you. Praying and witnessing His perfection in total stillness will truly leave you in awe. Embrace the dancing waves, the singing ocean, the clouds, the stars, and acknowledge His beautiful masterpiece. Never forget that God is literally everywhere, what a refreshing assurance of He who reigns.

Another way to pray is through prayer journals. Choose a notebook and pen you like or simply feel comfortable with and write out love letters to God, thanking Him, praising Him, honoring Him, glorifying Him, whatever you wish to write Him you can do so in this time. The best part about journaling is the way our mind releases its thoughts. It's almost like a sense of freedom for our minds to finally escape unto pen and paper. Documenting prayers also allows us to reflect and treasure our memories with God. Afterall, the journey is real.

Prayer partners is also another special way to pray. God says, where two or more are gathered His presence is all up in the atmosphere (Matt. 18:20 NKJV). Building and praying together, righteously brings joy to our heavenly father. As two are gathered His presence is strong within the midst, similar to the idea of another scripture, He shares that two are better than one (Ecc. 4:9 NKJV). Partnership breeds great impact! Imagine praying together and feeling joy by the presence of God. Imagine

God's army of angels intervening and interceding on our behalf, executing all things righteously. God's angels are the real move makers, and prayer in alignment with God's will is their role. God's angels are equally present as they are equipped and programmed to the sound of praise and prayer requests according to God's way. As we pray God's word, we become unstoppable. His word is a multipurpose tool for strategy, encouragement, comfort, and direction. God is pleased as we seek Him because He foresees the downfall in His absence.

Accountability is another special aspect to having a prayer partner. Because when one is low, the other can lift you high. The power of prayer is our sanity. The saying, *be about it, don't talk about it* comes to mind. Be about prayer, don't talk about the issues, dramas, concerns with the world. Share with God the highs and the lows. Share with Godly driven souls. Those who have our best interest at heart add value to our growth and development.

Above all else, prayer should be our first instinct, our daily exercise, and our daily bread. For reference, the book of Psalms includes one-hundred and fifty prayers that apply to our everyday lives. If you don't believe me, take a look for yourself. The book of Psalms is known to soothe the soul and restore hope lost. The holy word was designed by God so that we would believe in Him, know the truth, and be set free. God is our restorer and redeemer, through prayer He too is our deliverer. If you need a push to prayer, the book of Psalms is the perfect place to start, and yet expressing your thankfulness is powerful.

Keep in mind that prayer is transformative. Do not wait for life to go south, north, west or east to start praying. Use your prayer as praise. Use your prayer to stir good things within you, lift up your prayer to transform your life and the life of those you love. Just as God promises to bless us beyond measure, your praise can bless those around you.

Shout in celebration of praise to the Lord! Everyone who loves the Lord and delights in him will cherish his words and be blessed beyond expectation." (Ps. 112:1 TPT)

We are warriors! And the armor of God is our only true defense (Eph. 6:10-11 NKJV). May we dwell in God's presence and rely on His Holy Spirit for our every move–even in prayer. May we worry not and fear not the schemes of this world. May we put our entire trust unto the Lord, and rely on the Holy Spirit to direct us into righteousness. In Jesus' perfect name. Amen.

Giving thanks delights the Lord. When we are thankful and rejoiceful of who He is in our life, we deliberately decide to focus on the good. Our mind needs that. We need to focus our mind and whole being to the Lord, it purifies, it allows us to start afresh. As Jewels, we must make the initiative to pray, fast, and be thankful at all times.

But let the righteous be glad; Let them rejoice before God; Yes, let them rejoice exceedingly. (Ps. 68:3 NKJV)

May we pray over our mind, body, and soul, faithfully throughout the day. May we be covered by the strength of Jesus' blood that protects us in warfare and temptation. May we pray over our Jewel, from our head to our toes and every single organ in our body. With this being said, prayer is a muscle. Prayer is our weapon, while God our armor. Prayer is our strategy to connect, praise, honor, and hear God. Prayer is a weapon for all aspects of life as we seek stillness, holiness, and oneness.

Through life's journey, we will come to realize that prayer and fasting is the ultimate way to understand God's plan. Our faith is strengthened when we fast and pray. We grow in our trust and confidence in God. Most importantly, we begin to see how valuable we are and how perfect God's plans truly are. It is also important to fellowship with God's community of believers and build eachother up.

> But the fruit of the Spirit is love, joy, peace, longsuffering, gentleness, goodness, faith, meekness, temperance: against such there is no law. (Gal. 5:22- 23 KJV)

Maybe we have struggled with understanding the power and authority of God in the past. Maybe we have relied on sex to fulfill our voids. Maybe we have tried to pray and to no avail our reality needs some TLC. Still, God has not changed for He is the same today, yesterday, forever (Heb. 13:8 NKJV). And maybe we have just been going about discovering His wonders completely, all wrong. Perhaps we should at most seek God, give thanks. Truly seeking Him wholeheartedly is life changing. God is for us, and desires to reset our hearts and minds. Try God, and this will be the last day of uncertainty yet the first day of pure discovery.

Prayer will help you develop things you never knew about yourself. Some good too. Like the fruit and gifts of the spirit (1 Cor. 12:4-11 NKJV). As we delight in His fruits, we become fruitful. What a perfect scripture to pray and declare over our life. With each new understanding of scripture, praying it intensively and fervently will build our faith and trust with God. As we surrender, God gives us His unconditional love, joy, and peace. As we focus on seeking God and becoming more like Jesus, we will endure and conquer longsuffering.

Other Bible translations refer to longsuffering as patience, kindness, or forbearance. Transitioning and adapting to a pure lifestyle requires change. We have to be patient, kind, and forbearing, while change is manifested through God's Holy Spirit and acknowledging Jesus with faith and thanksgiving.

Prayer is a free tool to utilize. As reflected upon, patience is of the essence, for self and with others. We may miss the mark at times or many times when change is happening or when others may seem to disregard our growth, but God knows all. Rest assured that God sees our longsuffering and growth.

As we grow in your faith, we will become more fruitful. Your true self is flourishing and showing up. We become sensitized to God's way. God promises us that goodness and mercy will follow us through all of our days, in prayer thank God for His faithfulness. Pray that you may emulate God's character wherever and with whoever you are with. As we reflect on who we have become from where we came is purely by God's grace; we realize that we persevered through prayer because of faith in His promises.

Commune

> Restore us, oh Lord God of hosts; Cause your face to shine, and we shall be saved! (Ps. 80:19 NKJV)

Purpose is defined as the reason for which something is done or created or for which something exists; have as one's intention or objective. Commune is defined as a group of people living together and sharing possessions and responsibilities. The Bible shares that God orders for us to commune with purpose. God is our heavenly father, Jesus is our heavenly Savior. And fulfilling our purpose is effective with faithful communing and living in one accord. As we commune, we develop a pure heart and a sensitive spirit. Because of this, God's sharing of gifts, tasks, responsibilities are easily understood.

Communion is fellowship. Communion is a level of intimate fellowship that sets a tone for our heart posture. This intimacy is pure.

Acknowledging Christ each day is the way we purify our hearts, and establish peace of mind. A sound mind allows us to commune in peace and reflect with gratitude. Pure gratitude is natural in honoring a perfect being that willingly died on behalf of our sin.

Communion is sharing or exchanging intimate thoughts and feelings, especially when on a spiritual level. Communing with God is everything. God provides vision, purpose, and clarity. Our Heavenly Father loves us more than any other person, place, and thing. May we embrace God's love. May we embrace God's peace. May we commune with our creator daily to embrace more life, exchanging all our thoughts and feelings. May we embrace all of His gifts and goodness.

Our life is meant to be shared with God, our heavenly father. Our life is meant to be celebrated because of Jesus Christ. Communion is a special way to celebrate His life, death, and resurrection. We have been saved because of Christ's humility and purity. We are redeemed and restored because of His sacrifice of bearing our transgressions.

Jesus Christ allowed us salvation and for this very reason communion is the utmost respect of honor we can partake in as we reflect on his death. When we commune we honor reverence to Christ for his immeasurable sacrifice. We remember his life as we reflect on his blood and his body. We remember where we have been and where we have come from. We reflect on where we are in this precious moment because of Christ, covering us through each of our hard times.

Preparing for our day includes preparing a heart before God. Taking time to engage in Christ's crucifixion prepares us for hope and a future. Christ's resurrection is a part of a new beginning and songs of deliverance. Knowing that Christ exemplified the fruits of God's spirit is another aspect of communion allowing us to check our heart and align it to His perfect character.

Our spiritual preparation is communing with Christ who has rendered our path of holiness. Beginning and ending each day recognizing, honoring, and celebrating His significance in our lives is better than any television news report, social media like, or 'celebrity' post. Our real MVP, true and pure celebrity is the one and only Jesus Christ, God in the flesh. Our ultimate purpose is heaven, the purest place we will ever experience.

Believe

> Let the word of Christ dwell in you richly in all wisdom, teaching and admonishing one another in psalms and hymns and spiritual songs, singing with grace in your hearts to the Lord. And whatever you do in word or deed, do all in the name of the Lord Jesus, giving thanks to God the Father through Him. (Col. 3:16-17 NKJV)

A strong, healthy fear of the Lord is the beginning of faith. We must believe that we are capable of more success than more regrets. The ability to make the right choice is having a healthy fear of God and trusting His perspective. Right choices stem from wisdom, which stems from the word of God. We will lack knowledge as we lack God's word.

Acquiring knowledge sooner than later avoids a lifestyle of mistakes, a trend of impure decisions. Acquiring knowledge of God's word allows us to also develop faith. The word is living and active and as we pray as declared by God, we reap the benefits of His promises (1 Kin. 9:3 NKJV). Faith is the bridge we must be willing to cross to get from where we are to where we could be in God's Kingdom realm. Crossing the bridge is living in and on purpose.

God wants us to be the head not the tail (Deut. 28:13 NKJV). Being a light on the hilltop is by far more fulfilling than trending and blending with the crowd. Life with God is a fun, filled adventure. Focus is to believe in a better future, a better present. We must believe that our way has limitations; our means to control is exhausting. Having the same issues, complaints, and heartbreaks year after year is not God's way. We must pursue and desire more life. Surrender all control and let God do what he does best, change lives. Afterall, in surrendering our life, mentally, physically, emotionally, spiritually, financially, God's word speaks about the fullness of those who believe in Him.

> The Spirit gives life; the flesh counts for nothing. The words I have spoken to you—they are full of the Spirit and life. (Jhn. 6:63 NIV)

Gratitude and patience is a must. The journey towards purity requires a heart of gratitude and patience. Though with God we are assured that the journey is even more tranquil. To develop patience becomes an annoying (eager) enjoyment, the oxymoron is so necessary as we commonly hear "I don't have patience" but when it is a matter of becoming pure, this trait becomes all we desire. This statement changes to "Thank you oh God for your patience with me, thank you for gracing me with your patience and the peace to extend grace to myself and others." We can actually laugh and smile as people around us clearly lack patience and praise God for delivering us from that setback. We can happily observe these scenarios knowing Jesus is Lord and our day will carry on in victory as we count our blessings of patience with thanksgiving.

The levels to growing through this experience are fasting and sowing. Fasting is a spiritual, prayer focused discipline. God's goal for fasting is to exchange our physical might, purely for spiritual might. As opposed to relying on food to sustain us, He encourages us to rely on Him. In fasting, we surrender our hunger pain for spiritual gain. In fasting, we become undoubtedly closer to God than ever before, seeking Him for willpower and spiritual strength.

The phrase "I don't have patience" is such a sellout on becoming a better person. Developing a pure heart and righteous spirit are an enjoyable compliment. This combination goes hand in hand and will do our life good. Seeking God for pure strategy and wisdom is our significant key. Practicing the words *renew my mind, restore my spirit, uproot my ungodliness* are examples of initiating dialogue with our heavenly Father, specifically after praise and of course in exchange for what we don't have.

Acknowledging that we need to change, accepting that we need change, and actually adapting to change prepares us for greatness. Involving God is our daily routine strengthens the bond and relation. God is indeed our first love, though we have yet to conceptualize this fact. A strong, genuine relationship consists of intentionality, generosity, consistency, and responsibility. Commitment and faithfulness are biggies. In knowing this, God expects these same qualities in us; we need not to play Him, use Him, or abuse Him. Doing so is completely disrespectful.

With this being said, we can give thanks knowing that God is greater than any person, place, or thing. And by His mighty power and authority we excel no matter our circumstance. The beauties, gifts, and joys of seeking wholeness is in the eye of our beholder (Jm. 1:17 NKJV). God has literally spelled out all His glitters and glamours, leaving our faith to further discover His marvelous mysteries. When we are equipped and ready we stay equipped and ready. God fills our voids, and prayer and patience fill our uncertainties. We are in need of equipping ourselves with prayer and fasting. As we wake each day thanking God for life, health, wealth, and wellness, we embrace a new level of goodness. Prayer is essential in preparing and executing a fast.

To sow is essential to reap all the benefits God has ordained. Sowing requires patience, prayer, faith,. Sowing can be speaking life to others, planting seeds of righteousness, or building God's kingdom financially.

Influencer, Mattie James states, "I am more disciplined than I am motivated. Motivation is the cherry on top of execution. It feels good. But cherries aren't always in season. Discipline is. It always produces fruit." How timely!

Discipline is the key, while God is the master key in prioritizing our spiritual health. Producing fruit is a natural reaction to decision making. We decide whether we will produce Godly fruit or produce ungodly fruit. We have to choose, pick a side, like yesterday! There will be days we do not "feel" like being patient (BUT God), but we choose to be because of our heavenly Father's unconditional grace, and our devotion to Him. Being disciplined weighs more than feeling motivated. Being disciplined to love, pray, and fast, will do our souls well.

Reflection

- Are you ready to acknowledge, accept, and adapt to your greatness within?
- Are you ready to develop a new mindset, embrace a new strong spiritual mind, body, soul, and spirit?
- Are you ready to renew your soul?
- Write Galatians 5:22-23 in seven different Bible translations.
    - Amplified Version (AMP)
    - The Message (MSG)
    - New International Version (NIV)

- New King James Version (NKJV)
- New Living Translation (NLT)
- Living Bible (TLB)
- The Passion Translation (TPT)

But the fruit of the Spirit [the result of His presence within us] is love [unselfish concern for others], joy, [inner] peace, patience [not the ability to wait, but how we act while waiting], kindness, goodness, faithfulness, gentleness, self-control. Against such things there is no law. (Gal. 5:22-23 AMP)

6

FOCUS

Do not be conformed to this world, but be transformed by the renewal of your mind, that by testing you may discern the will of God, what is good and acceptable and perfect. **Romans 12:2-3 ESV**

Wow. This scripture is a favorite! The conviction hits hard. God is ordering us to not be conformed to this world, **no matter what**. He says do not do it, the loving warning is so clear and direct. Knowing we were born with a void absent of peace because if sin, He miraculously came to earth in human form as known as His son, Jesus Christ to become the newest, greatest focus (John 1:29 KJV). Perhaps, we can relate that sometimes we need to experience rock bottom in order to wake, we need to experience heartbreak to believe it. God said, well because of our stubborn and prideful nature, just note that being transformed will alleviate all the pain of the world.

God assures us that His word is living and powerful (active in other Bible translations), sharper than a two edged sword. With this being said, as we call upon His mighty name, He will draw near to us as the perfect loving, caring Heavenly Father He is. Because of His love and care, He has even graced us with warning and understanding. Whether we choose to honor His righteousness or not, it is our choice.

However, our life will be all the greater and better with His holiness. God's word is living and is the perfect guide for us to live, and embrace pure wholeness. We only truly benefit from the power of His word as we read it, meditate on it, and live it. God understands many will listen and not hear. Falling in love with self requires a genuine discipline to embrace God's creation, our identity in Christ, as well as purify our lives.

> For you, O Lord, are most high over all the earth; you are exalted far above all gods. You who love the Lord, hate evil! He preserves the lives of his saints; He delivers them from the hand of the wicked. (Ps. 97:9-10 ESV)

Aim to be different, aim to be better, aim to be bold. God created you to live and live life to the fullest. God created you to command His power and authority. We are more than conquerors, we are more than average, and we are more than sin. Be a light, be salt. We need to read His word daily, be fed by His Holy meal. We need to seek His Kingdom, be active in developing our purity. May we remain flavorful as we meditate on God's word and powerful as we live purely. God calls His beautiful souls to rise and be a light of this world.

In alleviating all the pain, reading God's word is the greatest assurance we will ever have. His word is equally necessary to the air we breathe. Only when we read His scripture do we gain wisdom. Our focus on God builds our spiritual strength as we rise with His word, eat His word, meditate on His word, and live His word. His wonders become clearer each day. Our spiritual strength builds pure peace. The strength of our spirit enables peace and ensures how well our heart is guarded. For instance, triggers or temptations that occur stem from a level of weakness in which requires a Godly assessment. The purpose of a Godly grind is ultimately purity and peace. Eternity is the sweetest, most delicious icing on top.

The struggles may seem to be real sometimes, but God's grace is more real. **Mindset is everything**, a Godly one. The reiteration of mindset and patience will have people questioning the three-hundred-and-sixty degree change. Why? When we are not conformed to this world, we stand out. When we are not conformed to this world, our mind is set on God and our assignment is clear. God calls us to be lights of this world, that we do not blend, that we are not dull. Being a light symbolizes strength, faith, holiness. A light also exemplifies goodness, knowledge, wisdom, grace, hope, and God's revelation. God's grace allows us to shine bright. God's grace renews and restores us. God's grace allows us to have dominion as we operate in our gifts, and walk in purpose.

In contrast, not being a light is darkness, despair, evil, not walking in dominion breeds insecurity. We can reflect on our present and past, and note whether our decisions or realities align(ed) more with brightness or darkness. We can also note whether we have been conformed to the ways of God or of the world. Darkness being a connotation of secrets, double lives, lies, where as part of our lives is hidden because of shame or disgust.

The great news is God saves the day, as He did two thousand years ago, yesterday, tomorrow, and will forever reign; God reigns. Do we focus on His way rather than our way, which has failed us over the years? Do we try God's promised perfection rather than rely on our flawed imperfection? Do we remain conformed to the patterns of the world, or be transformed by the renewal of our mind?

Transformation in Christ allows us to be tempted and not sin, hurt and not sin, broken and be healed, distraught and be delivered. Transformation turns mourning into joyfulness, poverty into riches.

Transformation is believing in God's miracles and reaping all His goodness. Transformation is a former prostitute, drug addict, pornography addict, child aborter, alcoholic being born again. Transformation is recognizing the darkness of the world and choosing to embrace the brightness, focus on the light at the end of the tunnel.

* * *

Conviction is a pretty pain. Pretty because need the accountability God extends us. Pretty because God extends His grace assuring that the thought or action is not right for our soul. Conviction is a spiritual confirmation that sin is real and an alarm for caution.

Conviction is also pain because we may still feel the remorse and shame of sin. The pain of knowing Jesus Christ crucified His perfect body, knowing no sin for the debt of ours. And yet we still bow to temptation. God needed our attention, secured it, and yet sin strangely can keep us in bondage. That's the pain, the pain of distraught being in bondage to sin, wrestling and fighting to live free with God as if there was no avail. Conviction allows us to focus on God with a repenting heart and turning us from sin.

Conviction sensitize our spiritual sensitivity and empowers the Holy Spirit within us. There is an unease of the soul as sin is near. The Holy Spirit is always game ready and His A game is just that, high class. The Holy Spirit assures us that sin is dangerous and that the decision we are considering is not beneficial. The feeling within our soul is strong of disgust perhaps causing us to cry or even vomit. This feeling is the first step in acknowledging our wrong, and the second step is to bow to God and focus on getting right. May we bow to God rather than bow to sin.

God graciously warns us that everything is permissible but not beneficial (1 Cor. 12:23 NKJV). Permissible being the leisure and freedom of choice to commit sin though in reality sin has never fulfilled anyone's void. Hence although sin is permissible the results are far from beneficial, a quick word from God. A quick, simple, profound word of wisdom does our focus and soul good. As we know the band aids of solutions have been tried, tested, and continuously run out.

Conviction helps us to turn away from sin as the Holy Spirit lives and speaks within us. This emotion of remorse occurs as we begin to focus on God, we recognize that we no longer have sinful desires. Through conviction, we realize that the Holy Spirit has indeed turned us away from sin which would have resulted in pain. This immediate encounter with the Holy Spirit is the pretty pain, which leads us to repentance. Only then when we repent is conviction pretty because we conquered sin. While the pain is crippling, fighting the good fight to be freed of sin's bondage.

However, shall we disregard our guilt and shame; we lose the gifts upon us. As a common lesson in life, we lose any gifts, persons, things that we take for granted in life. And equally people and things should lose having us as a gift if we have been taken for granted. Meanwhile, with God, our vision of focus equips us for the right people and things to involve ourselves with.

The Holy Spirit only thrives in righteousness. As we reject His guide there is no reason for Him to activate us with His holy gifts since we rather choose to live unrighteous. Taking advantage of our salvation is like a child that repeatedly abuses their curfew, or an adult that repeatedly cheats on their spouse. Someone is going to be mad, upset, hurt, and a lesson is needed to be learned. Submitting to Christ is showing up on time and committing to His holiness; additionally we have to respect His way. God's Holy Spirit is a gift.

When we focus on God we also realize that the purpose of sex was not meant to be casual, but marital. May anything not pleasing to the Lord be removed from our mind, body, and soul. God can turn anything meant for evil for His righteousness; we have to be focused on Him to reap His blessings. God is in the business of revelation; He will regularly reveal where our focus needs to be. May we pray more, trust more, focus more; focus to be a light.

> You are the light of the world. A city that is set on a hill cannot be hidden. (Matt 5:14 NKJV)

As believers in Christ, God, and His Holy Spirit we thrive. The power and might of His spiritual strength leaves us no choice but to focus and follow His lead. There needs to be leadership in our lives. We determine whether our leadership will be God or man. We determine whether we will focus on righteousness or unrighteousness.

Focus is purpose. What's life if we die with all our gifts and talents? What's life if we merely live, simply exist? What's life if we miss the joys of God's perfection? What's life if we aimlessly have sex with countless of people? What's life if we are only living for the next party to drink and forget? What's life if we continuously disregard our void?

Allowing God to be our leader discontinues our void. God is all knowing. Having a leader that is all knowing allows us to be prepared and primed for each day. Acquiring God's leadership takes faith and focus. While establishing a relationship with God takes time and devotion. As any strong, quality relationship, communication and consistency always wins. God's middle name is strength. He is naturally strong and of high, supreme quality.

God is naturally the master of strength; excelling in communication and consistency. Therefore, the responsibility is ours to match His fly. By matching His fly, step our game up or rather equally aim to communicate lovingly, with integrity. We need to focus on praying consistently with thanksgiving and for direction with praise.

> Light is sown for the righteous, and joy for the upright in heart. Rejoice in Jehovah, ye righteous; and give thanks in remembrance of his holiness! (Ps. 97:11-12 DBY)

To focus on direction is to focus on purpose. God is our idea giver (and please do not for a second question all the beauty there is to God, simply accept). He is **our everything**. We need not focus on the relationships doing us wrong, rather the one in the heavenly realm who only wants to do us right. Sadly we are also doing ourselves wrong and a disservice in our potential when we settle and stay settled. God gives us ideas in order for us to execute and fulfill purpose. Focusing our time and attention on His callings avoids the unnecessary detours.

To focus on purpose is to focus on God's direction of perfection rather than our own imperfection. Focusing on our imperfection supports the fact of *insanity*, if we continue doing the same thing and expecting different results. Well honey, we will never get a different result no matter the changed circumstance. Any situation or circumstance without God is already faulty. The highest possible potential has already been lost or discarded because of God's absence, God is indeed present wherever we go, as a child of His, we are responsible for acknowledging His presence and building our faith in Him.

Focusing on God's direction and acknowledging His presence can be done by prayer or praise. In order to achieve purpose we too need to understand specifically how to navigate; prayer and praise being beneficial in preparing our heart, mind, soul. In this preparation we can expect peace. Without focus on God, doubt and confusion arise.

Praying for direction includes understanding God's way, God's special way. In being the light that He has called us to be, His way is necessary. We already know we lack perfection; therefore there is no rationale in continuing on trying and failing at our own expense. Neither is it rational to become stagnant. The time of knowing that we lack direction is a level of growth, humbly so. No matter our age, we will never have it all the way together. That's why ding, ding, ding (smile), God's way is graceful and peaceful. We can be sure that refining our way with His will always beat the direction of our own *unintentional* demise.

Trying God will return great results as opposed to trying all things against Him. The trials and errors are long gone with our heavenly Father. God's trials are victorious and life changing. As oppose to trying God we may try sex or drugs, which only fills a void temporarily. Allowing God to intervene right here, right now will bring focus, structure, purpose. Allowing God to intercede will recreate the life we are meant to enjoy. Whether we are married with children or without, dating with children or without, or single with children or without, God's intercession will bring all the more joy. God will add the spice to life that waits. The mystery is marvelous. Try God. Live free with God, rather in bondage with the enemy.

> The Lord your God is with you, the Mighty Warrior who saves. He will take great delight in you; in his love he will no longer rebuke you, but will rejoice over you with singing. (Zep. 3:17 NIV)

As we focus on God, His focus is on us. With focus we acknowledge the magnitude of His gifts and blessings. Obedience to His way allows us to fulfill purpose, save souls, and build His kingdom on earth. God's kingdom realm is a piece of the void that we have been missing, and are able to experience with focus. Focusing on God will grant us all the goodness He destined for us. God provides more life, more joy, more peace, and more love. His scripture explicitly states He is the MIGHTY WARRIOR who saves! He rejoices, heaven rejoices as we devote and dedicate our lives to him. He already understands the struggles and insecurities of this earthly realm, which is why His plan for us was designed in His heavenly realm.

God is our Holy supplier; His word fuels our mind, His son Jesus Christ fuels our body, and His Holy Spirit fuels our soul (as well as faith). Spiritual strength is a game changer in this life of sin. The Holy Spirit lives within us as we focus our life on His lead. Faith operates as we trust God's spiritual strength and lead. He who gives us faith, and thus as we operate in the Holy Spirit we need to only walk with Him.

Operating in Him is all the focus needed to level up. Focusing on God also is having faith that He will never leave nor forsake us. At times we may need to grow through our own journeys for the betterment of strengthening a character trait, stretching our faith, trusting (surrendering wholeheartedly) God more. Be faithful in leveling up, and seeking to rise to higher levels (and heights) with God almighty.

Salvation is also a point of focus as we develop our purity and our relationship with God. Focusing on salvation is focusing on God's sacrifice He made for our sin. Believing in God is believing in all, absolutely all of His great creation and works. In accepting that He is the same yesterday, today, and forever brings peace of mind (Heb. 13:8 NKJV). We accept that Jesus died for us. Jesus paid the debt of our sins, and we no longer have to die for our sin. Oh so simple, yet such a huge rebuttal.

The simplicity of this acceptance is a matter of the heart. Truly believing that a human being was crucified on behalf of our wrongs is heartfelt, a sensitive moment for us to connect with God's Spirit and align with His spiritual healing. In this moment God's Holy Spirit also accepts the invitation of our acknowledgement to focus on a better life (Jhn. 8:12 NKJV). Focus is choosing to believe that Jesus Christ is the light of our dark world. We choose to focus on building our faith with our heavenly Father and in return are blessed beyond measure, while gifted with direction of Holy Spirit and cover of Jesus' anointed blood.

This acknowledgement does not go without mention of the rebuttal being our tempered and conflicted minds. Our minds have been tremendously affected and impacted by our personal upbringings. Many times we are unaware of the roots of cause that have shaped our mental health, which has also impacted our emotional and spiritual health. As our focus shifts, the impacts of our past become clearer. God has a way of revealing things that we used to tolerate or accept as normal for what they actually truly are. Revelation is the key in shifting our focus on life on God's holiness. God reveals the importance of fueling our mind, body, soul with His Holy word and spirit.

> You were taught, with regard to your former way of life, to put off your old self, which is being corrupted by its deceitful desires; to be made new in the attitude of your minds; and to put on the new self, created to be like God in true righteousness and holiness. (Eph. 4:22 - 24 NIV)

Seeking God's Kingdom is focusing on His word, Holy Spirit, and promises. Never minding what we have grown to believe in contrary to God's goodness, only when we are honest with ourselves will God still bless us one-hundred fold and beyond our wildest imagination. God asks that we put off our old self and unite with Him to embrace the fruits of His righteousness and holiness.

In John 15, we read an enriched analogy of spiritually maturing. God's creation has a special connection that enhances our understanding in the purest way. As we observe fruit trees, we notice that there are seasons they produce and others they are being nurtured. Their nurturing process is timely of God's natural springs of water, sunlight, and prune. Pruning is necessary for the growth of every living thing. God is also the vinedresser; He prunes, trains, and cultivates our vines. We have to abide in Him in order to be effectively pruned, trained and cultivated. As we focus on Him we develop conviction on purity, and become fruitful (Ps. 92:12-15 NKJV). God wants to bless us in abundance and team with us to win every game of every season.

Blessed are those who follow (trust) God with all their heart, and lean not on their understanding yet in all our ways acknowledge Him (Prv. 3:5-6 NKJV). This proverb speaks volumes of choosing God being simple, as the huge rebuttal is the reluctance in surrendering our entire heart. We tend to use God for certain aspects of our life and God is bigger than our limitations. This proverb also like each scripture speaks to other areas and seasons of our lives as we grow. God wants all our focus, not just part. May we turn away from our life and turn towards Him.

Focus requires absolute acknowledge of His will and His way that we are not swayed by the distractions of the world. Let's think about when sin originally entered the world with our fellow brother and sister Adam and Eve. The distraction of the enemy was deceiving and Adam's split second of focus on the enemy caused humanity their innocence. We need not lose not even the slightest milliseconds of focus on the enemy or he will capitalize on our weakness.

Wisdom

Choices affect our personal, professional, and relational relationships. Marriage is also destiny, the right person will bring destiny, and the wrong person will bring destruction. God's wisdom will direct us to secure the right friends, career, and marriage. Lacking wisdom will breed regret, discouraged by the friends, colleagues, and spouse we have. Wisdom allows us to make the right choices in our life. Wisdom is God's way of edifying our mind, body, soul, equipping us for His great masterpiece.

Wisdom from God is greater than wisdom from people. We either choose to focus on the perfection of His power and authority or the imperfection of mankind. Wisdom is power, the ability to change something. And God is power; He gives us the ability to change every situation. God will change our virginity status, relationship status, and emotional status. Wisdom is God's perspective. God's wisdom has been gifted to us in His Holy word. He graciously created His Holy word for our wisdom. As we read faithfully, we steadily increase in faith, knowledge, and revelation. Our relationship with others is a direct reflection of our relationship with God and knowledge of His word.

God is power. God is wisdom. And to live is to learn. To learn is to gain wisdom, knowledge, discernment. May God give us the wisdom to discern the relationships to maintain, purge, pursue. May God give us the wisdom to make the right decisions concerning purity and marriage. May God grant us wisdom for the way in which we should live, obtain great health, friendships, marriages, careers, and businesses. God faithfully reveals Himself to us in order to purely receive Him, receive His wisdom and word. The messages of the gospel are unlimited to wisdom, peace, love, joy, hope, sacrifice, humility, integrity, and strategy to equip us for everyday life.

Additionally, the gospel shares many stories of wisdom and the importance of praying and fasting. Our wisdom and faith grow as we pray and fast. Praying and fasting is leveling up in our spiritual journey. Desiring more of God, His supernatural spiritual strength is acknowledging that only by His spirit can we be the absolute best version of ourselves. Our focus shifts as our needs shift; our need grows as our wisdom grows.

The Bible says that we must not depend on milk but on His solid food (Heb. 5:13-14 NKJV). Prayer is our bread and butter, a part of our solid food preparing us mentally. Fasting is our water hydrating and purifying us from the inside out, preparing us spiritually. Prayer and fasting are to be depended on together in unison to equip us to experience what may seem impossible to man (and of course more than we can fathom), but is very possible with God. Maturing in prayer and fasting signifies that we do not rely on our flesh or food alone, but purely on the word of God (Matt. 4:4 NKJV).

Becoming spiritually mature is a lifestyle, and wisdom is maturity. We desire to know more of God's greatness, embrace more of His goodness. Praying allows us to intimately connect with Him and learn His voice. Being still, quiet and in tune with His command is important to hear God. Having a prayer journal and notebook for God allows us to organize His commands, while being good stewards and steadfast to the visions He created for us.

God's voice will lead us to become pure. God's voice strengthens our wisdom. Mentally, we are able to process our next move as well as prevent our next moment of temptation because of clear discernment. Spiritually, we are able to establish which parts of our character and personality need to be sharpened (this may mean strengthened and renewed or removed). As we become stronger in processing, discerning, and overcoming temptation we are indeed growing, becoming wiser.

Our heavenly Father is responsible for lifelong guidance, protection, wisdom, and love. May this moment be a time where we develop wisdom and discern God's word above all. We need God's wisdom in order to execute effectively for the purpose of glorifying Him in all that we do. As we focus on God who gives ideas, direction, and ultimate wisdom, our paths become smooth. Smooth, smooth. Our paths are supernatural.

Focus is power, wisdom is power. God is the supplier of both wisdom and power, allowing us to focus on becoming purer. Remember life is full of victories, let's make today the day we begin to actively, purely focus on all His goodness. Similarly to developing patience as we protect our jewel, the depth of patience becomes our new norm as we grow to nurture our Jewel with God's wisdom. God promises peace and wisdom through maturity, prayer, and fasting. Reading the Bible and praying the Bible is literally our means of focus to become protectors and nurtures or our precious Jewels. Focusing on turning the year experience into victory as God grows us through this season will be graciously rewarding.

> Sing to God, sing praises to His name; Extol Him who rides on the clouds, By His name YAH, And rejoice before Him. A father of the fatherless, a defender of widows, Is God in His holy habitation. (Ps. 68:4-5 NKJV)

As we focus on becoming wise, naturally we become pure. Wisdom knows that God we serve is greater than all other forms of love we may have tried and tested. Wisdom is striving to be a light because God's blessings are richer with a pure and sound mind. Wisdom is putting on the full armor of God (EPH 6:13).Living in darkness is bowing to sin, where God has already committed to being a father to the fatherless, a defender of widows, and our source of focus for all things righteous. No matter how long we have been in sin, sin as no track record with God. He simply desires our focus.

God scatters our enemies through faith, and fire (Zachariah 2:15). As we focus on seeking His wisdom, discernment, and direction, He makes a way where this is no way. The trust and believe factor are means to develop our faith and share the good news to the next soul. Renewing our life is not God's first rodeo, nor is it His first encounter with Satan's schemes as we note and reflect on Adam and Eve. They were God's first creation of man, shared in Genesis, the first book of the Bible.

Humility

Humility has been shared over a dozen times and now it is time to tackle this bad boy. Humility can seem to be a hard concept to process because we have been so estranged from God, resulting in living on our own terms, in our own way of doing things. To release having control produces a mental war in our heads. Most times we are unaware of this war because we have trained ourselves unbeknownst to be survivors and controllers. We need to control everything because we feel that is our only option.

Funny the word, humble has become like a fad, trendy word in some parts of our culture, though we are far from humble. People tend to pride themselves with being humble whether it be in a caption for a media post or as they boast in defense to the next person. Here is a great opportunity to actually be humble and reflect on how to be more humble. Maybe again, in *some aspects*, but the idea of humility is far from the natural eye. Humility is Godly, to be humble is spiritual. As we exhibit humility, we acknowledge our flaws and their hindrance in our life. We also acknowledge that we are nothing without God. We realize that our purpose is fulfilled with God's grace and mercy.

Humility is surrendering control of our life to our heavenly Father. Humility understands that we are always students in God's infinite classroom. Humility is accepting other men and women of God addressing needs for growth in our actions or characters. Humility is being graceful and remorseful when we are ungodly. To be humble is to quit justifying, over thinking, and opposing all the beauty there is to life, and its creator. Think, why would we exist to have no purpose, why would God teach the importance of humility if there was no greater purpose? Why would we have this precious gift of life, to die without embracing the fullness of the gift?

To be humble is defined as having or showing a modest or low estimate of one's own importance. As our greatest teacher who walked this earth, Jesus, His resurrection is the greatest teaching of humility. Jesus humbles Himself surrendering to God, acknowledging that God's purpose of that moment was far greater than another day of His life on earth. The heartfelt tears of writing and spelling this out are deep. The overwhelming thought of Jesus being perfect, God becoming a human to gain our attention and demonstrate true righteousness is pure love.

Jesus did not justify His ways of perfection, over think the pain, and oppose that God is still the Great I am. Jesus humbled his mind, body, soul, and spirit. He prayed and trusted that this act would bring Him closer to God. He realized that there was a greater good, and heaven awaited him. We are to walk like Jesus in all ways, by becoming ambassadors of Christ in aiming to become our purest self. After all, Jesus is Christ, God in human form. We must become humble, simple. And until then we will continue to fall short of all God's greater goods.

To focus on God is to focus on righteousness. God is the perfect, teacher, doctor, counselor, father, and friend. God's power is only revealed as we seek Him and then He returns favor in responding, confirming, and assuring. Similar to when we ask someone for a favor and they follow through, it is clear that they are listening and understanding our needs. God is graceful with favor over and over as He sees our diligence in striving towards purity. God is also patient with our confession and repentance. We need to surrender our heart to Him. These two acts are great measures of humility towards God.

> But those who love the truth will come out into the Light and welcome its exposure, for the Light will reveal that their fruitful works were produced by God. (Jhn. 3:21 TPT)

Integrity

> I leave the gift of peace with you—my peace. Not the kind of fragile peace given by the world, but my perfect peace. Don't yield to fear or be troubled in your hearts — instead, be courageous! (Jhn. 14:27 TPT)

When we are disciplined and committed to God, our focus shifts toward God. In Chapter 3, emphasis was made on our focus requiring a mind over matter approach in protecting our Jewels. The same concept applies as we completely immerse our mind, body, and soul with God. Although we have been consumed with sin, we need not to live in guilt or shame. Rather focus on God for healing and deliverance. As we humble ourselves in the sight of the Lord, we only care to live right by Him. Our efforts to be integral are owed to God for His endless provision.

Discipline is defined as the practice of training people to obey rules or a code of behavior, using punishment to correct disobedience; a branch of knowledge, typically one studied in higher education. In striving towards purity we need to be trained to obey God's word which are all the rules needed (Ps. 12:14 NKJV). His code is specified the Bible. While He communicates to us in various ways that are different. Though we each have privilege to hear His voice and are privy to dream, given our humility and commitment to purity.

God decides on how or when He will communicate for our attention, we need to have a discerned heart to His voice, and a disciplined spirit to His command. Punishment is the result of losing focus on His way which is the consequence of impurity. When we are in sin, God is the only correction, our fleshly nature has become too weak to have it any other way.

Pursuing a pure Godly lifestyle is a discipline, not a religion. God calls are to be disciplined and obedient to His word. Picking, choosing, and refusing how and when we are going to acknowledge His word or way is not cool. If we are not at the table there is no representation, the more we pursue purity, the more we become pure.

Commitment is defined as the state or quality of being dedicated to a cause, or activity. May we rise to every occasion with God, and pursue only causes with intent to glorify God. May we dedicate our entire life to His will. May we surrender our entire being with humility and honesty. And the spiritual cause of committing to God is salvation, purity and ultimately eternity.

Reflection

- Do you focus on overcoming challenges and embracing victories, or do you dwell on challenges and neglect your victories?
- What choices will you make today to persevere?
- What nurtures your soul?
- What changes do you need to make for Jesus to become your everything?
- Meditate on Psalm 92:22-15 for seven days. Memorize each scripture. Write it. Type it. Print it. Frame it.

7

MIND, BODY, SOUL

Love the Lord your God with all your heart with all your soul and with all your strength and with all your mind.
Luke 10:27 NIV

Choosing to love the Lord our God is a real big deal. Choosing to love the Lord our God changes everything. The way we breathe, think, feel, imagine, process, move, grind, plan, and focus. The joy and gratitude for each inhale and the conviction of our breath being a great gift is more or less breathtaking, a sweet crazy. Our heavenly perspective causes us to smile at the strife of everyday people who are in a state of stress, while we chill in a state of peace. Our imagination is purer.

He who literally provides for our every need and desire; the experience is humbling. God is our focus and we live to faithfully serve His kingdom and embrace His spiritual blessings.

God is wholeness. Loving Him with our entire heart is the beginning of obtaining purity. We must also love Him with our entire soul, strength, and mind. Our body requires His spiritual willpower as we grow through temptation. In growing through temptation we pray, fast, repeat. We read

God's Holy word to seek wisdom, discernment, revelation, and conviction. We equip our mind in that our love for God will not be compromised. Our relationship with God also sets the pillar and standard for those thereafter. Our relationship with God assures us which relationships need to be purged in order to live purer.

There may be a day we suddenly wake up literally from bed or simply in the midst of our step and realize that there truly is a greater being beyond us and beyond our greatest, wildest imagination. There is pure love in this being, our creator, who cares about our heart, our vision, and our relations. That trying God, choosing God is our destiny. We realize that God is our missing factor. Our hearts have been in void since birth, and on this particular day we reflect that our path has been lacking true purity.

Our reflection stems from the fact that our motives, intentions, thoughts, or purpose have been misled by physical will power. Some we actually have a spiritual encounter and an aha moment all in the same instance, no longer desiring to live on our own accord, but of greater means encompassing spiritual will power and strength. As with the matters of our heart, we either wake up and stay woke or we journey along life trialing and lacking pure fulfillment.

In loving God with all our heart, the peace is surreal. There are no trials and errors, yet pure lessons and victories. To be genuinely in love with God is everything, all our heart as ever longed for and then some and a whole lot more; His love is everlasting. Our hearts are filled with more than an abundance of His riches as He reigns over our life. In order to achieve God's goodness we must believe His goodness. Our vision is graced by God's divine intervention. Our natural gifts, talents, skills can only achieve their purpose of power alongside the creator who instilled them within us.

Jewel, Precious Jewel, our heart needs pure love. Our heart needs to be purified. God loves us with His entire being, we struggle with impurities and insecurities because we have failed to love Him back. His holy covering awaits our heart. His holy covering awaits our soul, strength, mind. God instantly covers, favors, and blesses His righteous disciples, disciplined to His way, the call. God is our heart's provider of peace, love, and joy. When we genuinely, purely love God with our entire heart with all that we do, He has our back no matter what. We no longer are orphans of the world, but servants of the Most High as our faith in God outweighs our fear in the world. In learning to believe and achieve, God calls us to be silent in His presence. As we are still and silent we gain spiritual, Godly perspective for every (and ALL) situation(s).

In experiencing God's love (stillness) and developing our Father-child bond, skin to skin contact is the epitome of purity. Remember the biggest game changer of all time, yes, from Chapter 3. God is the ultimate experience of pure love. Hashtag revolutionary. Well, in filling each and every void, from the little pieces of lingering roots of sexual immorality to the depth of loss, skin to skin contact makes an amends to these soulful disheartening. May we begin to unite with our heavenly Father in complete humility and vulnerability as we lay with focus on being still in His arms. God is our solution.

* * *

Our soul is naturally the purest part of our being. Similar to any natural being, until pollution or traumatization jeopardizes its wellbeing. As humans, we have been tainted and deceived with the distractions of sin. Unfortunately to a hungry soul every bitter thing is sweet (Prv. 27:7 NKJV). Fortunately, God has blessed us with this word of wisdom knowing all too well that we will hunger for His love, the pure honeycomb. While our pure soul hungers and thirsts to be connected with Him, in our sinful nature we cling to unrighteousness that may sometimes appear to *seem sweet*. Thankfully, God faithfully sheds light for our benefit.

Our soul longs to be pure and God longs to purify us. Gracefully, God promises to fill us with goodness (Ps. 107:9 NKJV). Our soul is a divine connection to the deepest essence of our being. The deep, deep wave of emotion that desires fulfillment is a soul desiring divine intimacy with its creator. We are soulfully connected to God's heavenly realm as we remove the wall that has been built through sin.

In humility, we accept that our souls have been polluted and traumatized over the years. In humility, we accept that our heavenly Father is our way maker, our purifier (Jer. 31:25 NKJV). And it is so fitting to transition from soulful matters to matters of willpower closing this section with, *"How are we going to win when we are not right within?"* (Lauren Hill). I'm believing God specifically ordained that lyric to purposefully be written here.

As we rest in God, our seeing, hearing, and thinking is clearer. Our visions are fresher, clearer, and more revealing. Because we rest in God, we naturally yearn and desire more and more of His gloriousness. As we begin to rest in His Holy name, we hear the sweet, sound of His voice saying, *I love you sweetheart, you are great, now get to work*, true word, true story as of today. When we desire more of God, in the heavenly realm of this sweet life, He prepares every necessary path. We must desire to love ourselves just as He loves us, oooh weee! #comeon #gamechanger. There are honestly so, so many game changers with God, He is the game changer. *Who feels it knows it.*

Okay back to business, loving ourselves the way God loves us, sit, think, and meditate on that momentarily. Loving ourselves, falling in love with self, the way God loves us. His love is perfectly undeniable, perfectly unbreakable.

Successfully resting in God is an experience. There are no words to describe the sensation. Being still and experiencing God's comfort and love is the best experience we will ever have while on earth. Our mind needs to be opened to the greatness of God, while our heart needs to be softened to the pureness of God. Currently, we have a lot of cleansing to do, ridding ourselves of the slanders, negativities, and doubts that we have been exposed to which causes mental hindrance. Cleansing also includes evaluating our relationships, and ridding ourselves of impure, devaluing surroundings.

Our mentality is valuable when fuelled with goodness though invaluable when not fuelled with goodness. How have you been fueling your mind, body, soul? Have you meditated on Psalm 46:10 NKJV? How can life be more restful, rewarding, and victorious? How can you love yourself better? Our mindset has a 99.99 percent (*fact determined through experience, and diagnosed by the author*) impact on the moments you experience. Fueling our minds with our Heavenly Father's word will ignite a fire within your soul that you contain or control. May we desire and receive more of God, while we desire to love ourselves more as well as aim to be purer each day.

Apart from acknowledging our unhealthy emotions through renunciation and allowing God to replenish our souls, the renewal of our mind is a factor of our mental and emotional healing. Our mind tends to dictate how the heart should "feel." Therefore, as we focus on being transformed by the renewal of our mind and discerned by the will of God, we will experience what is good, acceptable, and perfect (Rom. 12:2-3

NKJV). Our renewed mind enables a rejuvenating, pure soul and everlasting love.

Renewing our mind is so essential in embracing the fullness of life. Mindsets can make or break us. An impure mind is a result of sin and darkness which shape our mentality. We only do better as we know better and therefore if sin is all we know, sin is all we would do. Notwithstanding, we can look outside and equally admire the overwhelmingly beautiful sky. The difference is if we could equally admire the greatness in how beautiful the sky truly is. A dark, damaged mind cripples us, while a bright, renewed mind propels us. This mind is believed through Christ, and achieved with renewal of God's grace.

Renewing, restoring, rebuilding are spiritual focuses that support our emotional pain. Despite challenge, obstacle, or restriction, we are powerful beings, God's powerful being. We are capable of renewing, restoring, and rebuilding regularly by equipping our mind, body, and soul with pure goodness, God's goodness. Renewal is cleansing our lives to become more and more pure. Restoration is replenishing our souls to become whole. As we cleanse and replenish, God makes us new. God graces us with strategy through his Holy word and spirit for us to rebuild implementing His standards in our lives. God's principles allow us to maintain a sound mind, leveling us spiritually and emotionally.

Ultimately, setting standards, creating boundaries, having realistic goals allow us to renew, restore, and rebuild victoriously. Our boundaries also revolve around God's principles, and having sex without God is not one. And amen, by His grace we are forgiven as we repent and change. In becoming whole, Godly standards and boundaries equip us to make wise decisions. Realistic goals stem from God's will. Becoming whole, is becoming one with God, hearing Him clearly and honoring Him wholeheartedly.

It is important to clearly hear and discern God's voice in order to strategize, make moves, and solve problems while planting our seeds, sharing our faith. In strategizing, moving, and solving problems purposefully, our mind needs some strong renewal. It is neither not surprising the reiteration of unlearning and uprooting many of our mental flaws. We need to be made new. We need to purify our mind, body, spirit, soul. Purifying our mind is beginning to read the Holy Word and understand Godly strategies to soar in this life with the promises of heaven.

Oftentimes we must unlearn things we have been taught, and thus be active changers rather than active complainers. Complaining and blaming creates a deceitful heart. Deceit is concealing, misrepresenting and often time suppressing the hard truth. Deceit causes us to justify ill practices and prolong our delivering process.

Renewal in Christ is literally becoming a new man or woman. Renewal is appreciating the sweet revelation of God's word and promises and implementing His principles in our life. God's basic teachings redirect our focus and perspective on His righteousness. When we become sensitized to His word, we develop a conviction.

God is not only our foundation but also our restoration. We must also rest in God. We must rest in God to experience the peace and peak of self love. How exciting is it to know that God communicates to us as we rest. As we dream we have the gracious opportunity to connect with His love. Though there are levels of this realm, as there are in all aspects of growth. Only as we meditate on God's word, build our faith in God, and receive revelation of God's miracles may we be exposed to the fruits of Godly dreams. Notwithstanding that dreams may have always been God's love language with you or for a while though with a lack of faith and revelation, there will be a lack of understanding on the purpose of the dream. Through prayer and meditation clarity and wisdom can be achieved.

Jewel, Precious Jewel, God has designed us in the most precious, delicate, divine way. We are stronger than we think. God created us intentionally to become one with Him. Our strength and our mind are dependent on His spiritual willpower. God's strength becomes ours as we surrender our life to Him, physically, emotionally, spiritually. God miraculously orchestrates divine intervention as we seek His power. His strength is like no other. While fasting gives us the most crazy (good) supernatural power that figuratively can blow our minds.. Fasting is a blissful luxury, developing strength on the minutes.

With this being said, Christ's divinity is eternity. In becoming pure, striving to be like Christ we have eternal peace. Luke chapter ten stems from the parable of the Good Samaritan who asked Jesus what they must do to inherit eternal life. Jesus challenged the Samaritan to read the law, commandments, known as the word of God, and in doing as it reads we have eternal life (Lk. 10:25-37 NKJV).

God needs us to obey before He reveals. As He gains our trust on one level, He equips us for the next. And with this being said, having sex without God is disobeying His righteousness in living pure. Having sex without God is living in sin. While living in sin is putting (insisting that) our purity is in vain. God's focus is on our heart first and foremost, He is too great for ill intent. Thus, God desires us to entrust our bodies to him.

The choice to purify ourselves comes with God's blessing of spiritual strength. God gives provision for all things will too consent the blessing of our significant other; He knows best. Peace and love has an expiry date when fornicating and expecting more in life. Sin is ungodly, and thus not in alignment with God's blessings. Pure revelation occurs with pure obedience.

As an integral Father, He stands firm on His principle of trust. Trust is trust, while truth is truth. And we are familiar with this word , trust and the associated precautions all too well. Why then will we continue to place our trust with ungodly men and/or things, while our heavenly Father is the greatest trustworthy being? Although we may not physically see Him, we can spiritually trust and believe in Him. Our hearts and souls are dependent on His pure love, power, and strength. He created us and within us lays a vulnerable soul. Strengthening our trust with our heavenly creator is recalibrating our position before God. Our strength and value is symbolic to an eagle. May we understand our strength, value, and worth as we become purely, whole. May we confidently, purely own our size, strength, power in our God almighty, believing that it is He who provides our every need (Is. 40:31 NKJV).

* * *

Eagles are very large birds noted for their strength, size, keenness of vision, and powers of flight. God has created us equal quality, please let this marinate thoroughly. Better yet, let's digest this further as God could not resist the rise of excitement in digging and investigating deeper in the profound measure of this creature He lovingly created. Interestingly just yesterday, I smiled at God saying, "Is everything spiritual?" He assuringly replied, yes, as He is our spiritual, heavenly father operating in a spiritual, heavenly realm. And the story continues, the depth of the eagle is something serious. The motivation to research is all God; it's like a beautiful spiritual hunt for the real Jewel that will be the brightest light in fulfilling the purpose of Jewel, Restoring Hidden Treasures Through Christ. Let's resume.

Firstly, strength is the quality of state to be physically strong and the capacity to withstand great force. Secondly, size includes all the dimensions and magnitude of how big we are. Thirdly, keenness of vision both is a highly developed sense to see, and a sharp ability of wisdom to think, plan, and imagine the future. And fourthly, the power of flight is the ability to fly with power. God firmly says that we are to wait on Him to renew our strength, and that we shall mount up with wings like eagles; not to be weary or faint. Eagles also have massive curved beaks to break down and consume their meals, may we too break down and eat the Word of God with our heart, soul, strength, mind daily in our journey to purity.

Physically, eagles' broad wings (eight feet to be exact) and massive feet are perfect symbolic forces of who we are with God. We have spiritual wings to fly and conquer our destiny, flying and navigating above and beyond distraction, setback, and strife. We also have feet to move swiftly in God's heavenly realm, and embrace His kingdom on earth (Matt. 6:10 NKJV). God could only relate us to such a powerful creation as through His power all things were formed.

To fly is with one's own power, while the power to fly is without any outside influence. In knowing that God is our power, and He calls us to love Him with all our heart, soul, strength, and mind, why then are we disconnected from our power source? Why are we missing the opportunity to be happily pure, soaring high like an eagle? Without God we are air boarding without our spiritual power of influence. We are unpowered without Him, flying airborne, going nowhere without connection to our power source. Without Him we are operating contrary to His divine nature, unable to fly and soar as the *human-like* eagles He intended. As a result we are powerless.

Last, but not least, eagles are diurnal birds meaning they powerfully soar during the day, they are active in the light. As we love God with ALL our heart, soul, strength and mind, nothing can stop us, we are all the way up in the most absolute righteous way. May we rise and soar in the light from the dark path of airbourne we may reside.

> For what profit is it to a man if he gains the whole world, and loses his own soul? Or what will a man give in exchange for his soul? (Matt. 16:26 KJV)

Mind

Oftentimes our minds are consumed by the superficial *glitz* and *glams* of the world that we lose sight of purity. Our focus is consumed by the ill riches and "fame" of the world. We tend to strive towards lust and greed unknowingly until perhaps a moment of rock bottom occurs. God assures us that there is no profit in gaining the world in turn for losing our soul. Our soul is too precious, too valuable, too vulnerable to be exchanged for the impurities of the world.

Mentally, sex has become a part of our identity and is actually of crisis. Whether we pride ourselves having the most sex partners or having the "wealthiest/sexiest" partner, the intents and cultures revolving sex are disgraceful. We are unable to become pure, whole, as we pursue sex for all the wrong reasons. Sex is special, and we must relearn, refocus, and reset our mind in order to cleanse and purify our soul, mind, will, and emotions. Our strength is derived from God, once our mind has accepted that He is our pure source of power. When we believe in God's pure strength and wealth, the biggest gain we have is freedom.

We must be leaders of our wellbeing. We must be leaders and take initiative to understand, and execute strategies that are uplifting to our soul. Leading is moving mildly yet mightily. Leading is to overcome.

Leading is to become. Are you ready to become whole with God? Leaning on God is enjoyable and therapeutic. God is all we need to not just survive but thrive. Leading, fruitfully, joyfully, humbly, lovingly are pure characteristics to establish a better world, a better life. In establishing better, our mind has to make a conscious decision to part ways with sin.

Cleanse

Our heart needs cleansing, our soul needs cleansing, our mind and spirit needs cleansing. Seek first the kingdom of God and everything will be added to you (Matt. 6:33 NKJV). Jesus heals our sickness and forgives our sins (Lk. 5 NKJV). We are made clean with Jesus Christ. Jesus recognizes that we need to repent; He is ready when we are. God is ready to renew our sight, our hearing, our wounds, and our diseases (Lk. 7:22 NKJV). We have consumed an excess of junk. We fill our eyes with pornography, our ears with gossip, and our bodies with filth. We are a mess. Are you ready to commit to a pure lifestyle? Are you ready to level all the way up with Christ Jesus, Holy Spirit, and our heavenly father? Are you ready to be cleansed by the sins of your past? Are you ready to be purified and renewed?

Reader beware: Abstinence naturally cleanses the vagina or penis from its unclean nature. Abstinence also allows God to supernaturally renew the physical state of our purity, our secrecy. Our personal body parts are meant to be protected and nurtured. Protecting and nurturing our Jewel is a commitment of love, peace, and joy. Loving God, seeking peace in God, and embracing God's joy will render our discipline in taking care of our Jewel. Loving God and valuing His love for us will consciously cause us to abstain from sex that is not ordained by His will. God is fully aware that many will not abstain from sex in this manner; He too is aware that the gate to His Kingdom is narrow. With this being said, God will forever be God and life will forever be a gift. Though, with God, this gift is more peaceful and joyful.

Creating and establishing new Godly principles support our cleansing process. A new environment that is refreshing and appealing to our soul is also a wise move. An environment complimenting our Godly standards will also reduce or remove the level of temptations of sex, media, alcohol, greed. Our faith, trust, and security is within our heavenly father. The fears of missing out or lacking are inadmissible with God. Our faith in God prepares us for a Godly relationship, while our trust in God assures us that we are exactly where we need to be (right place, right time) and security in God embraces His healing and provision. Humbly surrendering our lives to our creator is the sweetest lifestyle. Humility is allowing God to have His control rather than allowing ourselves to take control, our means of control is flawed. As we recognize that God's way is greater than our way, the greater our faith, trust, and security will be. As we create a new environment, the things of the old will no longer serve us of the new.

A purged and cleansed life additionally refuses to stand for anything of no value. Embracing God's way not only cleanses us within, our senses such as lenses and tastes change for the better. No longer are we interested in strip clubs, prsostituiton, pornography and sex scenes on Netflix. These sins are convicting and alarming. We begin to question how our social life began to revolve around, sex, drugs, and alcohol, none of which is fulfilling. The more sex partners we have, the more disgust we pit. The more drugs we use, the more we become addicts. The more alcohol we consume, the more issues we face. Rather than chasing the next party, high, or sex scene, let's chase the goodness of the Lord.

Mental and spiritual evaluations are necessary, regularly. Evaluations can stem from the information being consumed, that is taking us further away from God's truths. While involvements can include *New Age* practices, happy hours, and senseless sex. Where God is not happily present, evaluation is essential. The spiritual battles/warfares/ties to these involvements will continue to attack our level of peace. Satan is gladly dwindling his way in doors that are open to him, whether known or unknown to us.

Cleansing allows us to embrace a new mindset, one of purely encouraging, and uplifting moments. We begin to be living examples of God's holiness. As opposed to exposing our soul to Satan, revealing our body parts, or flirting in our seductive nature, we remove ourselves from the spiritually conflicting and impure hype. As we draw nearer to God, we earnestly care to seek and discern His voice, as well as learn the gifts of His Spirit. With pure discernment, we clearly hear His voice.

Cleansing also allows us to be edified by the best relationship of our lifetime. Patience is a character that grows regularly. As we develop patience in learning how to protect our jewel, we too need to continue to master patience in learning how to nurture our Jewel. This work involved is purely rewarding as a jewel recognizes the fulfillment in glorifying God.

Walking in love, boldness, and strength is essential in achieving purity. Purging our life from the old may include emptying the fridge of alcohol, expiring "relationships", and removing gadgets and clothes that scream thirst. Thirst may be in forms of our clothes, character, and or communication. As men and women of God, modesty is the biggest fit. The thirst for sex needs not to be so real, rather the thirst for God, please.

Boldly sharing God's word and testimonials that has shaped our lives is like the circle of life. Supporting others on their journey is humbly, selfless. Others also have the opportunity to witness God's light amongst

His earthly body. Boldly speaking of abstinence and confidently living an abstinent life is precious. Security is plaguing our society. Sex "secures" us, media "secures" us, alcohol "secures" us, and greed "secures" us, though we are truly insecure to the core of our heart. As opposed to addressing and dealing with our lack of security we fill our souls with emptiness. By emptiness, temporary pleasures that take us further away from God and true purity. Hence, boldness in God is necessary.

The extremity of cherishing our inner peace is upholding purity at its finest. Sex is genuinely too pure, too sincere to be casually dipping and dabbing in for "hormonal" sake. We must not be afraid to speak on behalf of valuing our jewels. Rather, we must exemplify our spirit of boldness in restructuring and reestablishing our space. Our environment requires an anointing of peace, love, joy. Our environment too is precious and meant to be guarded and protected.

Clothes can be extremely revealing and limiting; the choice of trending with the next sex appeal top model or not is ours. Unfortunately, mainly females are victims of ill minded dressing. On the other hand males are aroused by the glimpse of an eye. The story unfolds, a thirsty male approaching an insecure female (or vice versa in terms of thirst and security) dressed in their sex appeal top model wear, while consuming alcohol. The only option on the menu is sex. Perhaps both male and female are dressed in the category below sex appeal top model, when alcohol is involved, the unfolding story is similar. The moral of these scenarios is that as we seek wholeness, we have to purge from sexual sin.

May the smell of alcohol cause our stomach to turn may the thirst of leisure sex cause our eye to weep. May we become more sensitive and remorseful to the ways of God. May we allow God to control how we dress, speak, think. May we be bold and secure in desiring more, the righteous way. May we understand that a new environment is good, great, and glorious. May we treasure and nurture our jewels for the sake of our children, future generation. May we realize that becoming new, being made whole is a journey of seeking God's love.

"There is power in the name of Jesus, power to save, power heal, power to change, power to lift. We are in desperate need of cleansing; God's power cleanses us as we submit to him. Submission is to love God with our entire being, choosing Him over impure desires. May we cleanse our beings to become in sync with God's goodness. May we humbly be in a state of repentance each day, as we are far off from Jesus' perfection. May we gracefully accept that we are made well, made better with our heavenly creator. May we embrace His cleansing from the crown of our head to the soles of our feet. May our eye gates be cleansed, may our ear gates be cleansed. May our thoughts be refined and strength be renewed. May we read, pray, commune more.

May our faith grow each day as small as a mustard seed as mighty as an eagle (Rom. 10:17 NKJV). God will never put us through life without His promise of deliverance. God is the producer and creator of righteousness. We may question diseases and pestilences, though God shares the causes of these realities in His holy word given our sin. God also lovingly shares the plan of the enemy; we need to hear, listen, and obey. In reading the word of God we are prepared and equipped for each day, each season. We are also aware of the measures of cleansing we are to follow in order to embrace His purities.

> No one tears a piece out of a new garment to patch an old one. Otherwise, they will have torn the new garment, and the patch from the new garment will not match the old. (Lk. 5:36 NIV)

In pursuing a pure lifestyle, we need not any lingering of our old life. All the newness is of our heavenly Father's revelations, principles, and miracles. God makes us new. God makes us whole. Lust and fornication has no business in God's kingdom.

> Do you not know that your bodies are temples of the Holy Spirit, who is in you, whom you have received from God? You are not your own; you were bought at a price. Therefore honor God with your bodies. (1 Cor. 6:19-20 NIV)

Body

Once we cleanse our heart, soul and mind as well as renew our thoughts, we can cleanse our body. This journey is a process of revival. Our body deserves all the restoration God provides. He is willing and able to exceed our expectations of wholeness. He is able to provide greater security than any sex affair. He is able to strengthen us beyond our imagination, beyond any temptation.

In loving God with our entire heart, soul, strength, mind, He desires our honor. In honoring God, He deserves our highest respect, and greatest esteem. He created us! Yes, as simply, marvelously pure as it gets. God created us intricately, forming our most inward part, all our parts. The detail in knitting us together precisely in our mother's womb. We are fearfully, wonderfully created by the gentle touch of His command, by the perfect breath of His majesty. We are God's masterpieces of a great, perfect world, His world. Our bodies belong to Him. We were created by Him, for Him.

Wherever we go, there the Lord shall be. God follows us, leads us, covers us as we return in the pureness of His arms; the purest place we could ever fathom. As the Lord is pure, created us pure, so shall we live. We were created to be pure, live pure. The way we think, speak, and act. The way we conduct our entire body reflects who we serve. As we serve and honor God, our dress, our posture, our approach has a standard of purity. God orders our footsteps as we hear, listen, obey.

Our footsteps are made pure as we hear God clearly and obey immediately. In hearing God, our ear gates need God's necessary cleansing. To hear God steps back to being cleansed by God, and steps further back to choosing to love God with our entire heart, soul, strength, and mind. Only then can we pray boldly, tread boldly, and reap boldly. Only then can we hear clearly because our heart, soul, strength, mind are conditioned to His source of power.

Bold prayers ensure soulful and spiritual restoration (ACTS 4:31 NKJV). Praying boldly as another asset in developing our spiritual strength simultaneously develops our faith (II Cor. 7:4 NKJV). Seeking to be made new in Christ and building our faith is everything our souls have ever desired. Jesus promises us that our faith saves us.

Tiphani Montgomery has also shared that, "as Jesus' bloodshed and body broke for us, we instantly received the perfect blood transfusion." Always so timely, she proceeded that, "God cares to give us open heart surgery with the blood of Jesus." Amen. May His surgical works begin and flourish. God desires to deeply purify us, while surgically transforming us. The depth of this significance is revolutionary in the most compelling way; we owe every inch of our body to God. By this, even as we commune in revering and honoring God, may we acknowledge the sentimental value of Jesus' blood. May our minds also process and understand that we are because Jesus was, God is.

Soul

> In the same way you received Jesus our Lord and Messiah by faith, continue your journey of faith, progressing further into your union with him! (Col. 2:6 TPT   )

Jesus loves us, this we should know. Jesus died for us, for our salvation and freedom. Jesus is the son (born) of God, the human replica, while His Holy Spirit exists and lives within us. We have the opportunity and ability to thrive. We are privy to experiencing heaven on earth. We are privy to being made new, pure. Jesus has already laid our cornerstone. His blood is our spiritual anointing, which covers and protects us in our everyday path. Each day is a new beginning, and blessing to grow closer to our heavenly Father, be more like Jesus, and be led by the Holy Spirit. We must test His Spirit as we relearn to live purely, Godly. Our faith is built as we execute the Holy Spirit's guide, as to fulfill God's will. God will always confirm and assure us in His special way (sign) as a kiss of heaven. Devotion is having a healthy fear of immersing with the Lord God, with pure focus on His Holy Spirit.

Baptism

> If anyone desires to come after Me, let him deny himself, and take up his cross, and follow Me. (Matt. 16:24 KJV)

We are made new in Christ resurrection; we have a new life in Christ because of His sacrifice on our behalf. As we desire, we give up our selfish way, and take up God's way. In denying ourselves humbly, we confess our sins and in our heart, soul, strength and mind we love and follow Jesus' perfect example. God's Holy Spirit works within us as we desire to follow Him. We become a part of the body of Christ, in pure harmony.

The bible speaks of three baptisms. First, spiritual internal baptism. This initial baptism occurs when we accept Christ within our heart, repent, and receive the gifts of His spirit. We are saved by grace through faith. It's spiritual, nothing physical (Jhn. 3:16 NKJV). Second, physical external (fulfill all righteousness) publicly declared to the world. Water is an outward expression, symbolism of purity, and sign of death and resurrection. Water shows the world publically our act of faith and commitment to God (Acts 2:3 NKJV). And third, immersion with the Holy Spirit as we are supernaturally baptized with our heavenly tongue which is a level of spiritual surrender with a physical utterance.

> I indeed baptize you with water unto repentance, but He who is coming after me is mightier than I, whose sandals I am not worthy to carry. He will baptize you with the Holy Spirit and fire. (Matt. 3:11 NKJV)

Baptism is a spiritual encounter of purifying and cleansing our lives. As we immerse ourselves in the pureness of water, God has ordained an anointing as a symbolism to wash clean our body from sin. As we immerse ourselves in the pureness of the Holy Spirit we are graced with His vocal gifts, revelatory gifts, and power gifts (I Corinthians 12 NKJV). Thank you Prophetess Tiphani Montgomery for your Kingdom Entrepreneur University (KEU) teachings. We either embrace a poor life of lack, or a rich life of fullness in God, His heavenly realm. Baptism is a level of spiritual growth as we move in the dimension of spiritual gifts and seek purity. According to John 8, God shares that we are to be baptized in the Spirit in order to operate in His Spirit such as embracing heavenly dreams and seeing visions. Our gateway to heaven is an eternal fulfillment; while present we enjoy benefits of being a Christ follower with the spiritual gifts of baptism. Heaven is eternity, while the world is temporary. Seeking purity is seeking heaven, prioritizing eternity.

Jesus said to him, "I am the way the truth the life. No one comes to the Father except through me. (Jhn. 14:6 NKJV)

Reflection

- Read, Luke 10:27 and pray daily. Seek pure wisdom and revelation.
- Search mustard seed in the Bible and record each scripture that includes this term or refers to this term.
- Read the word of God daily, throughout the day.
- Pray the word of God, throughout the day.
- Study the book of Acts for greater revelation of the Holy Spirit.

8

GUARD YOUR HEART, PROTECT YOUR PEACE

As for God, His way is perfect; The word of the Lord is proven; He is a shield to all who trust in Him. **Psalm 18:30 NKJV**

Guard your heart, protect your peace. This is an essential daily prayer. This spiritual sword equips us for dodging the bullets of the world. Whether a colleague is sharing their drama, the government is always pursuing corruption, the news is always portraying negativity, as a firm believer of God who reigns we are shielded by His guard and protection. To consume ourselves with all the impurities of people and the world will set us up for failure. As soulful beings our heart and peace are precious. Jewel, Precious Jewel we were created for a pure, soulful relation with our perfect heavenly father (Jhn. 15 NKJV).

There's greatness inside of you. Are you ready to acknowledge, accept, adapt to the greatness within you? Are you ready to develop a new, strong mindset? Are you ready to embrace a renewed soul? When we are equipped and ready for greatness we will remain equipped and ready to climb mountains. Choose God's love today, commit to pure self love, and embrace a true spiritual wellness journey. In choosing self love today, perhaps focus on achieving new fitness goals, building a new business service, and preparing delightful plant based dishes.

Jewel, precious Jewel we are fearfully wonderfully made. We are to celebrate ourselves, big ourselves up for who we truly are before God. We are to love ourselves the way God does rather than the way society or media says we should. As we embrace the joy we are in God's eye as precious jewels, we embrace the will of divine purity He has to release our struggles mentally (emotionally), physically, and spiritually. Fulfillment is bred as we first accept our brokenness and desire more, accept God's offer of trailblazing. Our journey may be tough initially though it is worth the fight.

Focusing on the good more than not so good symbolizes maturity. God is all good. In growing our relationship in thinking more like Him, visioning more like Him, believing more like Him, acting more like Him requires a particular grind, living fearfully and wonderfully (Ps. 139:14 NKJV). The Hebrew word for "fearfully" is *yare*, meaning "to be afraid, stand in awe, fear." When used by an exalted person, who is our heavenly father, it means that we are to stand in awe. Standing in awe is a natural response as God guards our heart and protects our peace, graces us with true purity.

Focusing on God is to focus on His goodness. Psalm 139:14 implies that we have a great reverence as well as heart-felt honor, interest, and respect for our heavenly creator. God created us this way. We need him, hence our void as we have been living without Him. Living without God is missing the fullness of His goodness and the revelation of His peace. If our days pass by with a lack of complete awe in the stillness of His presence, we are losing all the way out.

To be "fearfully" made means to be "awesomely" made." The word fear has a connotation of fright in the world, though God intended for us to have a joyful fear of Him, a loving, healthy fear. As our creator, He created us to understand who the real boss is, who was in charge then and who is in charge now. Similar to the demanded respect of our earthly parents, lovingly so. No matter what age we are, our parents naturally, extract a level of authority in their sweet sternness. Our parents most likely raised us to respect their household. As children, even if we were to cause trouble, receive punishment, disobey rules, we still longed for our parents' love and affection. The fear instilled was and has always been to teach moral and morale.

Our heavenly father raised us in our mother's womb and the pure meaning of fear is to develop a heart of awe in His presence. God raised us with similar, yet greater morals. God raised us to live in awe of His perfect creation. God has raised us fearfully and wonderfully, while no weapon formed against shall ever prosper. He has our back for real, fo' real. He has our purity as His best interest at heart. God causes astonishment and inspires all things perfect. His heavenly being can seem unbelievable as we move further from Him, though believable as we draw nearer.

Our focus on God builds our spiritual strength as we rise with His word, eat His word, meditate on His word, live His word. His wonders become clearer each day. Our spiritual strength builds pure peace. The strength of our spirit enables peace and ensures how well our heart is guarded. For instance, triggers or temptations that occur stem from a level of weakness in which requires a Godly assessment. The purpose of a Godly grind is ultimately purity and peace. Eternity is the sweetest, most delicious icing on top.

Our grind with God is a beautiful, deep experience. A Godly driven (focused) grind and maturity in faith allows us to develop our purity. While, a Godly focus enables a pure, Godly lifestyle. God's focus is peace, and He guides us too to focus on peace within. Inner peace blossoms over time as we stay guarded from sexual desires and immoralities. And internal strength ignites external strength. As God's focus is peace, and our focus is God, we too experience pure peace. God is our Prince of Peace, our Protector of Peace.

Additionally, God's spiritual strength is our guard. Striving to be pure, is to be more like Christ, less like our self (our sinful nature). Striving to be pure is to trust God as our shield and guard every day, all day. God is our strength to say no to temptation, and yes to righteousness. As we are convicted by His word, including His teachings and principles, our heart posture changes. His ways slowly but surely become our ways. God's standards are our way of living.

> Have I not commanded you? Be strong and of good courage; do not be afraid, nor be dismayed, for the LORD your God is with you wherever you go. (Jos. 1:9 NKJV)

God is a strategist. Many times we may in actual fact be in a situation that screams endurance. In these instances God may very well be using us to build us in a way unimaginable to prepare us for our next season. In preparing us, He challenges us to be a light where there only appears to be dark. Our mindset is always in making the impossible possible in either saving His lost souls or glorifying His Holy name by His grace. We are walking Bibles and in some instances the only purest version the world may see.

Guarding our heart is a strong mechanism in soaring like an eagle. In overcoming the world we must take on the world, guarded and protected. The world is full of nonsense, toxins, lies, and evils. Being guarded is a force of spiritual wisdom that allows us to protect our peace. For instance, we may have a happy place, sitting near the ocean, in the grass, on a mountain top, or flying in the clouds, or cruising on a boat. Our happy place is a sent of peace and joy, in the presence of God. Peace is being in the midst of chaos and fear, but God the perfect being we serve causes us to soar above. Peace is smiling, saying chaos who, or fear where? The contentment we experience in God is as a result of eating His word, purifying our lives, and guarding our souls.

> Then the LORD your God will restore your fortunes and have compassion upon you and gather you again from all the nations where He scattered you. (Deut. 30:3 AMPC)

Faith is also purely built by reading and hearing the word. And in reading the word, we realize the simple, yet strong measures in becoming pure. The importance of being pure is well for one, God himself is pure, and then two, purity enables peace. As our faiths build, means of spiritual protection arises. Reading, believing and praying the word of God, game changer on all levels. No one can tell us anything as our security is in heaven.

As we read God's word, we read the promises He has set before us. We realize that our life has pure meaning. We are part of God's creation to enjoy and embrace the fullness of His love. God is everywhere, He exists wherever we are. In reading His word, we begin to appreciate the magnitude of His beauty. We begin to appreciate the magnitude of our existence. God only wants for us to be saved, however He too understands that sin has plagued His earth. With this being noted, He assures us that the battle is not ours but His alone. Reading His word is comforting, encouraging, assuring. His grace is sufficient for all, though He understands that not all will live to their purest potential. God's love for us will never end because He created us.

There are times when children and parents in the world and our community have conflict and issues. It is hard for anyone to understand how a child could disacknowledge their parents. Many times there is hurt and trauma. And the child struggles to forgive and heal from the implications of their parent and child relationship. The child continues to live and grow further away from their parent(s), even though they birthed them, and raised them.

Congruently, there are times where parents also disown their children for various reasons, and therefore the child's idea of God is tainted. This tainted idea of God is impacted from an angle of neglect, as our natural response is to blame. Because of our emotional pain, we actually blame God for abandonment. As we question, why would God allow this pain to happen?

In respecting that we each have a choice and the decision is not always pure, or righteous, other people are affected. Unfortunately, we may be the person affected as a result, though fortunately we will always have God's help, love, and unwavering peace. God is a perfectionist in turning a not so good situation into a great situation. Not allowing God to heal us, exposes our heart to the enemy's deceit. This deceit causes the mind to overthink, resulting in dwelling and being burdened by our past. As a result we delve in impure activities believing them to help our brokenness, meanwhile Jesus was sent to heal the brokenhearted (Luke 4:5 NKJV).

> I will lift up mine eyes unto the hills -- From whence comes my help. My help cometh from the LORD, Who made heaven and earth. (Ps. 121:1-2 NKJV)

In these cases God is the perfect being to draw near to. Even as a parent in this predicament, drawing near to God will also render forgiveness and strategy to overcome (Ps. 34:18 NKJV). Only God truly understands our pain. Unfortunately, He knew that the time will come or separation or complication between parent and child. He knew this would be a testimony that would save another soul given the strength we endure as we chose to rely on Him.

We all have a choice to make, good or evil. And in good there are levels to it, in choosing righteousness to please God or choosing unrighteousness to please self. Our faith is what saves us to secure salvation. Just like any math problem that equates to give us a solution or product, God is our missing component or factor to every equation in order to solve every problem. Although there may not always be a grand problem, God is still the factor needed to enhance, design, and develop each strategy.

Sometimes our pain is so real the idea of even trusting another being seems far-fetched. Though, it is important that God be our first resort of protection and peace. He will never leave, forsake, or abandon us. God knows our past, present, future, as we may have experienced in the past. Because God created us He is able to fulfill us permanently, and in filling us we are guarded and protected. With God creating us, He knows the extreme delicacies of our heart. It is only right that He who knows us, guards us. As we allow God to guard us our faith becomes stronger and stronger; our peace becomes stronger and stronger.

God is our source of all things. Running to guard our hearts and protect our peace is a part of the joys within His heavenly kingdom. We have indefinite protection, peace, strength within Him. In dealing with sexual immorality, the way we overcome is by acknowledging on God, and allowing Him to direct our path (Prov. 3:6 NKJV). God will never direct us towards mindless sex. God will never direct us towards abusive relationships. God will never direct us towards masturbation.

God being our source of all things means that His source is greater than every scheme of the enemy. Someone that desires to protect us from harm will not put us in harm. God is too righteous for any means of nonsense. We only need to trust and believe that His way is greater than our way. Meanwhile Satan prides himself in conflict and destruction, knowing when as we do not have peace he rips our heart out, spits on it, and throws it near the furthest desert. When not in one accord with God, we are naive and idle. We become susceptible to a heart in the desert. God is spiritual, and so if we are not the disconnection is real. In building our peace, we need only to activate His Spirit within and connect with His Holy language, prayer.

Praying our way towards purity is the purest vitamin needed to begin this journey. Praying is a vitamin that needs to be supplemented in every aspect of our life, and throughout each part of our day. Praying soothes the soul, cleanses the mind. Praying provides clarity where there is uncertainty. Praying helps us to declutter the mind from our natural way of over thinking and over processing. Praying is a form of God's therapy, as we talk with Him, commune with Him, and honor Him, He spiritually responds. The calming of the soul ensures that God hears our outcry and whisper.

> And the peace of God, which surpasses all understanding, will guard your hearts and your minds through Christ Jesus. (Phil. 4:7 NKJV)

Peace is real! God is real! The realness in peace is the sweetest joy unimaginable. We cannot process it because we have ways to go in cleansing, healing, and renewing. However, God is there every step of the way delivering us from the mess we have accumulated, while uprooting every piece of sin within our soul. A deep clean to the soul allows our hearts to be readily available for God's seeds of righteousness. God's seeds release purity. As our hearts are spiritually guarded by God's unbelievable force, yet so believable because He is God. Once we truly acknowledge that He is our almighty God, our hearts are faithfully guarded and our peace is protected.

Guard your heart Jewel, precious Jewel. May we not be a slave to sin. Our sinful nature's goal is to destroy us, while our spiritual nature's goal is to build us. Our peace is precious. Guarding our heart is equally important in living a holistically healthy life. Therefore we are to activate the Holy Spirit within us to embrace the peace that transcends all understanding and allow God to protect our hearts. Because God is peace, though we may never fully conceptualize this supreme idea, we are protected by His spiritual might.

God's word is the script. His script is all we need in this life of sin. His script changes the game, our source to develop purity and gain wisdom. We can be full of gratitude knowing that God is greater than any person, place, or thing. And by His mighty power and authority we excel no matter our circumstance. God restores, changes, and transforms us. His ability is willing and able, what may be impossible to us is simply possible to Him.

Accepting a Godly lifestyle, is accepting a life of greater heights. Leveling up is a part of this new norm. God stretches what we believe to be our *strongest* or *greatest.* He stretches us because we are capable of more and we are deserving of more, more life, more freedom. Our faith will be tested, our hearts will be tested, our peace will be tested, and though having complete assurance in God will prepare us for each season of our journey. And we will testify with God's almighty power, our faith is tested to build Godfidence, our hearts to build resilience, and our peace to build patience. Living Godly is living purely with a clear focus of having a guarded heart, protected peace.

Sing

God provides us a new song, a new dance. We instantly are graced with the love and pureness of His warmth. As we seek Him, He is right there to extend His open arm around us. Singing is a sweet therapy. Praising, worshipping and honoring our heavenly father to the sound of His prophetic instrumentals compliment our time in His presence. God acknowledges our praise as pure gratitude for His majesty.

Maintaining a state of worship edifies our soul and ignites our peace. To sing is to express our love for our heavenly father. To sing is to express our gratitude for healing, joy of contentment, and excitement for eternity. Singing God's scripture brings our worship to levels. God loves our heart of worship; He is all up in the space. As we are at home in the shower or on the move in the streets, God rejoices with us as we honor His Holy Name.

Singing also becomes a part of our spiritual journey. Our lifestyle of purity is enhanced as we fuel our heart, soul, strength, and mind with the goodness of His prophetic music. Each choice we make is categorized

Godly or ungodly, when we reflect on the music we consume the categories are simple as simple as God comes. The math factor here is to subtract ungodly music, or add Godly music to add value to our walk alongside God.

God's healing flows as we sing, praise, worship. His strength surpasses our imagination. His strength enriches everything, from security, relationships, marriage, to rest. Worship covers our insecurities and naturally and spiritually boosts our confidence. Our relationship(s) and marriage is restored through the growth in discipline and prayer. With spiritual clarity, Godly decisions are made also with confidence. We rest in God's presence as we sing as soon as we rise until we soak (enjoy skin to skin contact) before bed to rest. Singing God's praise is a norm that adds to our favorable victory and supernatural healing.

Singing gives God permission to flood our mind with goodness and causes the enemy to flee. Singing guards us amongst others; we are guarded by scriptural music. In the instance we get a flat tire we can rejoice and smile knowing that nothing can spoil our joy, though as we become in sync with God's complete anointing. He covers our relations and assets. Perhaps as a tire does flatten, the greater good is testifying the greatness of the Lord to the person nearby while sharing God's faith.

May we be hungry for everything God wants for us. Purpose is God's preference for us. May we go to God who gives us vision and seek that He clearly reveals it to us. May we be humble to accept God's specific direction in order to make our greatest impact. In order for God's preference to become our experience it requires our participation. This experience also requires an honest desire as we seek to rest in God's presence, God's nearness, and God's glory.

God specifically aligns our vision to talents and interests He naturally gifted us with. Fulfillment is of God; fulfillment is peace, love, and joy.

We have to have open conversations with God and pursue what is truly right. Inner fulfillment is greater than outer *fulfillment.*

May we be faithful that the darkness we are in will become brightness with God, that our conflicts will be resolved peacefully, righteously in Jesus name. And may we understand that the Spirit does not wrestle against flesh and blood yet against the principalities of this earth(EPH 6:10-20 KJV). We actually need God on our side, because the spiritual battle and warfare is overbearing without Him. God is willing to guard our hearts; we need only to be willing to allow Him.

May we dwell in the presence of the Lord. May we dwell in the unconditional love of our heavenly Father. May our heart be pure, our soul be pure. May our mind be pure, our body be pure. As we develop intimacy with our God, may we be pure in embracing His perspective. May our senses become one with His. May we experience His tenderness, warmth, and affection? We must not want anything to do with making choices in our life, but want everything to do with God's choice for our life. And with this heart posture, pure protection and peace manifest in our lives. As we believe, we achieve.

And lastly, though never least, as we embrace God's forgiveness, protection, and peace, may we have a heart of forgiveness. We heal as we forgive. We reap peace as we forgive self and others who have wronged and inflicted pain upon us. Forgiving others and healing self leads to wholeness. By the blood of Jesus we are made new, this we must decree and declare. Being destined is greater than being damaged, while spiritual revelation is also greater than general information. God works with us as we work with Him. We know peace as we know God; we are protected as we no longer dwell on being neglected.

9

EMBRACE SEXUAL PURITY

Let no one despise your youth, but be an example to the believers in word, in conduct, in love, in spirit, in faith, in purity.
1 Timothy 4:12 NKJV

Our means of control has gotten the best of us and we have lost sight of our value. Embracing purity is embracing our value. Our true value stems from true purity. God created us whole, created us pure. As we entered the world sin sadly has ripped us apart. Our soulful parts are tied to Tom, Dick, Jerry, Henry, Joe, Boe, Tim, Bombquisha, Sally, Sue, Jane and the list goes on. We have failed to protect our Jewels, precious Jewels.

We are to deal with our past relationship dramas and traumas because the root of these issues will continue to grow deep. Roots of drama and trauma will always hinder and affect each relationship until spiritually conquered. Sex is spiritual, yea that's right. Residue from these relationships will naturally continue to tread lightly with us because we have conditioned ourselves to choose a temporal, quick break (sex fix) sexing as opposed to choose an eternal fulfillment. We have chosen to stuff and ignore our wounds by chasing the next high. At times the high is sex, while other time the high is an actual substance that further abuses our beautiful soul.

Alcohol is the devil. Alcohol is a poison, no matter which way, angle, turn we aim to justify its taste, it serves no purpose in our bodies. There is no glory from drinking alcohol. Our breath stinks horribly, our mind is disillusioned terribly, our liver is affected greatly, and our earnings are shared unwisely. Alcohol literally has no benefit to our precious beings. In one way or another, the mind, body, soul is impacted by its cause of altering our natural, pure state.

Sex and alcohol have both become a part of societies norms. Societies glorify the next big alcohol brand, while communities arouse off of the next "big" party where the alcohol is unlimited. "*Eww*, gross *smh*!" is the exact sentiment when we realize God's peace, love, joy is unlimited and we shamefully have chosen the former over the years. Repentance is of the essence. Prayer and repentance will soothe the soul. Seeking God's comfort is gold and supports our healing journey.

Abstaining from alcohol is to simply embrace the sweet smell of dark chocolate, pure water ,the ocean, fresh air, or any other natural goodness in its purest state. Choosing to prioritize our purity, wiser choices are essential. Prioritizing our purity equips us in developing great health. Knowing that alcohol has no health benefits makes the choice in consuming this substance ignorant. The choice of something having a negative impact on our mind, body, is a soul perishing in *la la* land.

Oh and notwithstanding the by-products of intoxication. The unstable decisions that result from drunkenness is by far avoidable if our choices stemmed from wisdom. Consuming alcohol leads to drunkenness which leads to sex. Most times there may be regret because of the irresponsible order of events that had taken place. Other times a child is conceived in an irresponsible and unhealthy space. There is a running apparent "joke" to some that a *child* is their *birth control*. Rather righteous standards and wisdom is a purer mentality.

Sexual abstinence is a measure in becoming pure, whole. Abstaining from sex is choosing to become physically pure. We owe our bodies, our precious jewels greater care. The value that we truly possess is diminished by each sexual encounter. Regaining our purity is disciplining our minds to focus on our worth, committing our bodies to God, applying mind over matter to embrace the strength of God. Without relying on God's spiritual strength we become weak from our physical strength, resulting in entertaining our temptations.

In purifying our mind we learn the importance of engaging with like minded communities and building wisdom from God's Holy word. In becoming pure, our heart, soul, strength, body is equally in need of thorough cleansing. We are to reassess and reevaluate what adds value to our lives and what subtracts value. As we abstain from sex, we cleanse from the sexual roots that have grown over time. We are responsible for removing negative, sexual relationships and adding positive, spiritual relationships. Providing that abstinence is a struggle because of past issues, developing and maintaining Godly roots within His word will give us an unstoppable mentality.

Mentality

> Beloved, do not imitate evil but what is good. He who does good is of God, but he who does evil has not seen God. (3 Jhn 1:11 NKJV)

Firstly we must get our soul right. Second we must get our mind and body right. Our souls are not subject to society, they are subject to God. Because society may glorify or condone sexual immorality, we need not to adopt this mindset. Society construes our mentality for the worst. Society has a way of portraying unrealistic pictures and instilling fear. Unrealistic pictures may be the timeline in which one must be married with family, the type of body one should have to be considered attractive (or even this idea of sexy - that's a whole *nother* book), the "pure" fun we have as we consume alcohol. Fear is instilled as surrounding media share bias thoughts based on their one sided perspective. Without God, there will also be fear. But with God, peace is the greatest form of mental health.

In getting our soul right, the word of God is our means of direction. God's word truly is the purest source and script to live by; we need only to give it our purest try. Our soul is fertile either producing seeds of goodness or not. We choose what we consume our soul with, whether we desire to produce fruits of righteousness or unrighteousness. Our soul gets rights each day as we fill our soul with God's prayer language and word. Ungodly sex does not get our soul right. We have to believe that we are worth more than mindless sex. And then we can achieve a purer mentality as we abstain from sex.

Similar to fasting from food being a discipline to rely on God spiritually, abstaining from sex is a discipline to rely on God mentally. While in both of these processes of cleansing, we are too strengthening our soul. As we purify our mind and body, our soul is naturally edified by God's Holy Spirit. The traction of force is like a magnet, becoming a soul with dignity, respect, honor of self, Holy Spirit supernaturally activates within. God's spirit instantly connects with our soul as we align with His purities. God continuously operates health checks, going to and fro each life assessing our spiritual alignment with His (2 Chr. 16:9).

In getting our body right, praying and fasting are truly the greatest practices to focus on. Disciplining and committing ourselves to these powerful experiences will allow God to supernaturally infiltrate and change us from the inside out. Jesus assured His disciples that faith in His will allows them to conquer and overcome all things righteously. Abstaining from sex will too require faithful and faith based prayers. Our bodies are delivered and purified in pursuing sexual purity, while having faith in God's divine plan.

> So Jesus said to them, "Because of your unbelief; for assuredly, I say to you, if you have faith as a mustard seed, you will say to this mountain, 'Move from here to there,' and it will move; and nothing will be impossible for you. However, this kind does not go out except by prayer and fasting. (Matt. 17:20 NKJV)

God's love is a whole other kind of love, far from ordinary. More like extraordinary. Who feels it, knows it full and very well. His love is filled with miracles, signs, wonders, and promises. He promised us authority to take full dominion right in the beginning (Gen. 1:26 NKJV). How special is this! How great are His signs, and His wonders! His Kingdom is everlasting and His dominion is from generation to generation (Dan. 4:3 NKJV). Therefore it is only right to respect God's power and love, for sin shall not have dominion over you, for you are not under law but under grace (Rom. 6:14 NKJV).

As we meet our future husband or wife, God is with us, never letting go. And a quick side note, God's natural creation is for a man and a woman to become one in marriage union, opposite sex, not same sex by any means (Lev. 20:13 NKJV; 1 Cor. 6:9-11 NKJV). Like any sin, we must be delivered from all ungodliness in order to inherit all the pureness of His kingdom. God desires to strengthen us, teach us, join us in marriage, raise our children and empower us to be great.

Throughout our years we have conditioned to certain aspects of life that are actually not in alignment with the word of our Heavenly creator. The rational we cling to is a justification of our upbringing or living environment. While some weaknesses we have are unknown because we have adapted to the normalcy of our circumstances. These situations are due to a lack of wisdom and Godly driven motives. There is also the reality of apples not falling too far from a tree. Unfortunately, relational cycles are common, though not God's will. God is gracefully awaiting the moment we decide to break these curses as we seek His will and way. God's face is the purest, most *beautifullest* part of our singlehood.

Being single is the most admirable season in life. God strategically orchestrated singleness to grow and blossom. Being grounded and secure in who we are takes time, effort, and discipline. Our time is precious, precious jewel. Our time is meant to be wholesome. In becoming pure, becoming whole, we have to embrace every single aspect of our single season. We are to spend time learning self, building self, and securing self.

In learning, building, and securing, our focus needs only to remain on God. We know how to love as we love God, because God is love. We know how to build as God graces us with power, purpose, vision, strength, because God is power. We understand security as we align ourselves in God's image, because He created us in His perfect likeness, God is perfect.

We are amazing single beings. No other being qualifies for our own *amazingness*. We own our pure, true quality, state of the art precious Jewels. May we truly honor God with our body in this season, in Jesus name. May we truly value our identity in Christ. There is a special kind of growth that takes place when we invest in our relying on God wholeheartedly rather than a relationship. There is a special kind of fruit produced as we allow God to nurture our souls.

Taking etiquette time and effort becoming pure will allow the following season to be even more fruitful. If we are damaged with spoiled fruit so will our relationship be. As we establish a disciplined, Godly lifestyle our focus is so strong. Our self esteem is high because of our confidence in God, and our confidence is one *hunna* because we understand our greatness, pureness before God. And as my beautiful First Lady, Lesley Osei would say, "know who you are , and know whose you are".

In a recent Instagram post by a woman of God, Heather Lindsey she states, "Find the beauty in your current season. God has you there for a reason." There is reason in each season. Our heart has to be so pure to align to the callings God places for us, because if not we may miss it completely. Whether there is a lesson to be learned, a business to be built, or an investment to be acquired, being single is a part of life's journey. Being single is Godly as He challenges us to learn purity at its finest, while tests our heart (Deut. 8:2 NKJV).

Included in this same Instagram post from Heather Lindsey, she set the record straight for all the singles, stating, "The grass always seems greener on the other side." While single, there may be moments of wishful thinking, discontentment, or disappointment because we "feel" that we *should* be in a dating relationship or married. This saying of the grass seems greener stems from a lack of peace.

Lacking peace is lacking quality time with our heavenly creator. The grass is rich in greenness as we focus on becoming pure and feeling whole given the strategies of prayer, fasting, cleansing. God provides for our every need and there is purpose for each of His seasons. Praying and fasting for pure contentment needs to be our main priority.

Meanwhile, we need not to be solely seeking a relationship for sexual motives. A relationship has a physical purpose, and spiritual destiny.Additionally our personal relationship with self as a single person has purpose . Having ill motives such as sex being our sole intent requires developing deeper ground in God's word as well as within in His spirit. Sincere motives and intents are formed as we are centered with God. With a relationship (or marriage) seeming to be the greener side in this case, the single has self checks to grow through.

Purity is embracing God's steadfast love above all, because as we do, we are synchronized and sensitized to His desire for our life. Purity is choosing to sustain from sex until God's blessing of marriage is clearly revealed and accomplished. In the beginning, God created Adam and Eve, man and woman. Well, actually, He created heaven and earth, though speaking of the origins of mankind. Our fellow great, great, great, great, great, great, great, great…grandparents were God's original creation of human beings, the pure representation of a Godly marriage operating in complete nakedness. Not by absence of nudity but by openness and unashamedly, which is absence of sin.

God blesses two to join as He did Adam and Eve. Females were the last human form of God's creation, while males were the first. At this time, Adam expressed his appreciation for God's creation, Eve. This example is of the perfect marriage relationship. Therefore a man shall leave his father and mother and be united and joined to his wife, and they shall become one flesh (Gen. 2:24 NKJV).

Men are commanded to appreciate women and lead their family, while women are commanded to respect their husband. Affirming, loving, and pushing each other into our destiny is necessary. Marriages thrive as both man and woman support each other. Marriages thrive as both man and woman are secured in who they are before Christ, who God created them to be.

Security is developed during singleness and edified during marriage. Singleness is a personal time of intimacy with extreme sentimental value of becoming one with God, establishing God as the cornerstone in our personal life. God desires for us to become whole as we are single in preparation fulfilling destiny acing marriage. Providing that we are not whole in our individual seasons, we are not in alignment with God's will.

Are we ready to become whole? Are we ready to become pure? As we reflect, wholeness is a gift received as we live pure. Purity is a gift as we live Godly. Wholeness is a pure state of being, having a perfect heart before God. Wholeness is a pure understanding of our power and authority in God. Wholeness is to understand that God is our cornerstone. Wholeness is to know that God completes and harmonizes us in perfect peace, that we are whole as we whole as we unite in His love.

And although sex takes place in marriage, God's purpose of bonding couples together is unfulfilled shall He not be the cornerstone. God created relationships and they are are meant for two to gather as one and produce a greater good. God has designed marriages for His glory as all His works, that we value and respect His ordinance. God has predestined marriages to radiate among the nations, living and shining in His honor. Yes,God,God,God. As marriages live according to God's will, their multiplied impact tremendously builds His Kingdom. God is a multiplier by nature and designs His stories for the purpose of multiplying effects in order to save souls.

Celibacy

Sex is God's creation and ordained for a special, Godly moment. Many times, we misuse and abuse our body for the sake of temporary fulfillment. We have misused the purpose of sex and abused our jewels, precious jewel as a result. Although we tend not to reflect on the purpose of sex or the purpose of our life, God has created a perfect, beautiful moment for our purpose to be exalted in His perfect time. God's perfect timing is too the best time for us, though we have yet to surrender everything to His will.

Abstinence may seem unreal, and unreasonable because it is not part of our cultural norm. Though what about all those who actually are suffering emotionally, mentally because of the countless, ungodly soul ties and heartbreaks. At what point do we sensible address the cause of premature sex. At what point do we protect our jewels from further hurt and disease. Having sex with different men and women will never fill our void. Even relying on our husband or wife for sex to "feel" better or fill our heal any wounds is unhealthy. Sex is not meant to cure pain, stitch wounds, or escape reality.

Our goals in life have been skewed. Our focus in life has become corrupted. Having sex with multiple people in a lifetime was never God's plan. Once bowing to sin and disregarding that we are jewels, precious jewels, we diminish our value. We lose respect for our own person and the sex game accelerates. We lose the standard of our profound secret parts and intercourse strips all innocence. As we lose our innocence our heart naturally becomes hard, while overtime harder and harder. The fact that the "special" or not special someone who takes our virginity is not our first and last is problematic.

God's design for sex is intimacy. Sex is a gift, equally to celibacy being a gift. These gifts are both rooted in God's divine design. Given that God is our spiritual, heavenly Father, we too have a spiritual purpose. As we marry, only then are we to embrace God's purpose of sex intimately with our spouse. Otherwise, we are to embrace the gift of celibacy. There are further purposes for married couples as there are for singles. There is a divine purpose for each divine season God orders for our life.

> Preach the word! Be ready in season and out of season. Convince, rebuke, exhort, with all longsuffering and teaching. (2 Tim. 4:2 NKJV)

God is always using us to glorify His Kingdom. As we are in need to be found by His righteousness, celibacy is a gift that is needed to be glorified, celebrated, honored. The glory in pornography, stripping, prostitution, fornication, and relational drama is in desperate need of shifting. This shift requires an exposure of bringing these dark encounters to the light. This darkness is a messy spider web of impurity and will keep us webbed and entangled with sin without recognizing our gifts in sexual purity. Our stories of our sexual immorality season are meant to be shared, and souls are meant to be saved as we shed light on God's word, teaching others the joyful power in purity.

Sexual immorality consists of impure thoughts, desires, and actions. Whether friends with benefit status, exchanging sex for income, intimately involved in a relationship, faithfully watching porn or leisurely masturbating, God is crying for our embrace. Our souls are being lost throughout the streets, figuratively so. We must fight this spiritual battle that attacks us in thinking impurity is not harmful to our well being. We must fight this good fight releasing our souls of ungodly ties.

Ungodly sexual Soul ties are deadly. These ties result from sexual intercourse and the exchange of the mess from another being inflicted upon us. *Say what? Mmmhmm.* May those unclean, ungodly soul ties be rebuked in the mighty name of Jesus, our saving graces' name.

Why do we self sabotage? Why do we cause pain and hurt upon ourselves? Why do we hinder our sacred place to ill spirits? Why is celibacy frowned upon? Why is sex trending? Why do we inflict ourselves with unhealthy relationships? Why do we sacrifice our precious jewels?

Jewel, precious Jewel, God did not design sex to be painful and hurtful. God did not design sex to be exposed on television and celebrated before marriage. Embracing abstinence is a part of developing purity. Embracing sexual abstinence is a part of being made whole by God. God's way will always prevail because He created us. There is no other true way of establishing wholeness without our Heavenly Father, and with Him creating within us a pure mind, body, soul.

> For in Him dwells all the fullness of the Godhead bodily; and you are complete in Him, who is the head of all principality and power. (Col. 2:9-10 NKJV)

Worth

God has created us for victory (Deu. 20:4 NKJV). We are deserving of all great things and perfect things. Blessings after blessings are promised to be ours as we acknowledge our value before God. Life is pure, free, and whole as we firstly, intimately connect with our heavenly creator. Life is purely sweet as we understand our worth and power in our father God. We are priceless; a jewel, precious jewel.

In embracing abstinence, we develop focus and wisdom. We value God's purpose for our lives and understand our worth. We embrace God's security daily rather than security in sex. Our worth is like a jewel, precious jewel of high class, prestige value. Sometimes we believe that having sex will make someone love us more, make us popular, or give us the child that will *truly* love us. With our new focus, a Godly perspective we realize the value of sex is marital and not casual. We recognize the gifts of celibacy, and the gifts or Godly ordained marriage. We also recognize that the purpose of sex is for marriage intimacy, not casual lust.

With this being said, Jewel, Precious Jewel, we need not to be having children aimlessly. In knowing our worth, we value the worth of our children's destiny. Our children are destined multi-millionaires, billionaires, innovators, creators. Our children deserve love and affection by both parents, who are in union and love each other. Our children deserve all the structure and strategy to live their absolute, greatest life. Without structure and strategy their destinies are affected and their greatest potential can be damaged.

When there are broken families and broken homes the child suffers. However, suffering is avoided with God as well as addressed with our heavenly Father. Again, He is our peacemaker. As God fills our voids, (and yes, this is a daily doing) our families are enriched. Strength of nurturing and fostering a child established within a home is infused by a Godly lead. Life is real, and real, real as different circumstances arise, whether the death of a parent, adultery of a parent, or illness of a parent takes place. These circumstances can too be a matter of the child.

Failing to identify our worth in God, our unconventional circumstances can turn from bad, to ugly quick. Godly lead families allow us to cope with managing brokenness. Broken families can consist of single parent homes or grandparent/guardian homes where the mother and/or father have been removed from the home equation. This too may mean a child's relationship with a parent is nonexistent or severely sabotaged. Broken families can also be married families whose unhappiness is absorbed by children (or a child).

Not only is the development of a child as they are young children affected, but as a child becomes a young adult. Deep roots of trauma, rejection, and insecurity plague tremendously. Many times these roots are unknown until certain situations arise, i.e. relationships that become unstable or are not meant to be pursued initially. Many times we can also be immune and accustomed to trauma, rejection and insecurity believing it to be normal and simply our worth. And the cycle continues. At times parents can tend to me unaware, consumed by their issues and neglect the impact separation tolls on a child. Or even a child may be consumed with issues unbeknown to the parent. Establishing our ground within God gives us spiritual wisdom and discernment to address family matters. Our individual worth, family worth, is worthy to God.

And by all means, products of both of these environments are amazing. These children grow to tell a story, these parents equally share an incredible story. God steps directly in the middle of these situations and establishes His throne for glory and sought. Other times, God rescues and saves a parent or child within these situations and the dynamics change tremendously, praise God! As we recognize our worth, He comes through for the win. God makes single homes well, co-parenting homes well, broken homes (abuse, pain, suffering) well. Let's imagine God within the picture from beginning to end. Imagine God truly leading our marriages, homes, children, finances, emotions. Imagine surrendering our entire beings to God, and what a sweet life it will be. Hashtag, wholeness.

Relationships are meant to be open, free, and vulnerable. We need this with God, as well as our spouses. Our relationship needs to be recalibrated to the word of God. Blessings and promises of vulnerability are fulfilled when we are truly with the person God intended for us. May we be purposeful, peacefully. May we be vulnerable and victorious. May we not give up our worth for nothing, rather live according to His divine design. May we know who we are before God, and whose we are.

Reflection

> For this is how much God loved the world—he gave his one and only, unique Son as a gift. So now everyone who believes in him will never perish but experience everlasting life. (Jhn. 3:16 TPT)

- Read 1 Timothy 1 (Homosexuality)
- Read 2 Timothy 3 (Righteousness)
- Read 2 Timothy 4 (Awareness)
- Read Colossians 2 (Wholeness)
- Read Romans 8 (Hopefulness)
- Meditate on Deuteronomy, spoken by one of God's prophets named Moses. Listen via the audio Bible, it's a great option.
- Confess the name of Jesus fervently and command His boldness.

10

REFLECT

So all of us who have had that veil removed can see and reflect the glory of the Lord. And the Lord—who is the Spirit—makes us more and more like him as we are changed into his glorious image.
2 Corinthians 3:18 NLT

Trusting in other people who lack pure wisdom to develop wholeness is similar to trusting in the desert to maintain hydration. And depending on the desert to thrive is like depending on our own physical strength. (Jer. 17:5-11 NKJV). Purpose is our pure gift to life, our value in the world around us. God is purpose and has created us on purpose, for purpose. God created us perfectly, purposefully. As we read more, learn more, we are able to change the globe (originally rapped by Nas). Though, God is the *Original Gangsta*. With this being said, reading the word of God is our means to learning how to change the globe.

God is order. In changing the globe, His divine order and structure are our standard for purpose. Particularly changing the globe is referenced in this case as our communities and families. We all have a reach in which we can either influence positively or negatively. And in positivity there

God calls us to live righteously. Choices opposed to living Godly are unrighteous or mediocrity. God has established an order for each of us to execute our purpose, righteously. His order also includes reaching and loving souls in our sphere of influence. Our reach is a part of our purpose, and is far from mediocre.

God created us to thrive in Him and depend on His Holy Spirit and spiritual strength. In relying purely on God's power and strength we become powerful and strong. Our quality is pure. Our quality is one of a kind. To discover and embrace purpose is to discover and embrace God, change our ways. Purpose stems from purely understanding our identity in Christ, not man.

Our purpose is fulfilled as we reflect and delayer the scabs of hardness that have dried over time in our sinful nature. Receiving God's supernatural power allows us to overcome sexual desires and relationships; change for His glory. As we recognize that God is present within, our soul catches His flame of holiness. This flame begins to penetrate and purify us inwardly, then outwardly. Family, friends, significant others are incapable of penetrating our souls, filling us with God's power. Only our heavenly father can fulfill a great work within us, enabling us to produce good, pure fruit.

Our fruit stems from the flame within and carries throughout the world. All the power, every single bit of control belongs to our heavenly Father. God makes what may seem impossible possible. Everything is possible with God and every part of our purpose is of Him. We learn our purpose from our powerful source. Wholeness is a gift received as we live pure. Purity is a gift as we live Godly.

Sadly, we have become tumbleweed rolling with the wind and their punches, there is no purpose given a lack of trust unto the Lord. Our purpose to live is rooted in God. Our reason to live is for God. We long to live for Him, to become one with Him. Our trees eventually dry out and dry up without God. We begin to worry and become affected by the world around us. We consume the mess because we have no root or source of nutrition. Droughts prolong seasons of scarcity while rivers our everlasting water. God is so cool how He creates nature to connect with, and purposefully creates perfect analogies to shake our head in amazement.

A perfect heart knows they lack nothing with God, in God we have everything a source for all things, all things righteous of course. We are to take God's word and apply it into our life rather than take our intellect and apply it to what we think to be *life*, should be life. Why not intently ask God, who created our life, our purpose. God's perception is greater than our perception, which breads our purpose. Our heart must be true and of pure quality to receive His discernment to execute His perfect intention.

We depend on what's written in God's word in order to be purposeful. We depend on God's perfection to repair our roads of sin, heal our wounds of insecurities. Because the enemy is anti-Christ, wounds of insecurities quickly result in anxiety, depression, and darkness. The sins that are a product of these emotions hinder our progress in achieving our true, pure purpose.

Sin and purpose does not mix. Well, they are not a nice mix as this combination is similar to drinking outdated dairy milk (and if we have yet to accidentally consume this, *try it for context*). The purpose of this liquid to complement our cereal for a great use turns useless in seconds. The primary purpose of our life is to complement God's creation. And our secondary purpose is to make our mark on earth, our specialized impact of greatness. Greater is He who lives within thee. Our God and our purpose are indeed the greatest mix.

Furthermore, the attempt in achieving our purpose while pursuing sin is like swimming in the dark. First, sin is extremely dark and our state of being lost is of the essence. While second, the chance of drowning at night is a very great, great percent, likely *one hunna*. These mentioned emotions are intentions of the enemy. While God is of purpose, Satan is of anti-purpose. By any means necessary, Satan will aim to oppose God's perfect way. Destroying and causing destruction in our lives is Satan's purpose.

The fact that we have become neutralized to sin is the fact that we know no different. As we choose purpose, we choose to reevaluate and reassess aspects of our life that complement our purpose or not. Purity is highly censored, meaning the clarity in our lens changes slowly but surely. Our taste buds even change, yes regarding food (cough cough plants are life) though also our taste for relationships and commitments. The only entitlement we humbly have in this precious life is choice. For one, we choose either to listen to sex driven (secular) music and desire more sex or we choose to listen to Godly (worship) music and desire more of God. Each choice is ours to make to walk in purpose or to walk from purpose.

Purpose is being serene and calm (Jer. 17:7-8 NKJV) knowing that God is our source of life. God penetrates our tomorrow as we reflect to be more like Christ. Temperance with the Lord is a fruit of His spirit, a reliance of God allows us to strive towards purpose joyfully. Our faith and belief in God weighs more than our faith and belief in man. Our true hope is God who sustains every need, our given purpose.

God has planted an internal ease that is truly an external strength, God's gift to us. "Our gift is operating to our fullest potential, our God given authority" (Montgomery, T. 2020). God is our traction, He is our consistent force. Without traction to God, we are unable to consistently move in purpose. His grace allows us to be magnificent and miraculous;

these are external strengths when route it in God's goodness. Our consistency and tenacity is driven by God, given His internal ease. Purpose is peace.

Many things are not worth our time or energy. Learning to remove what is not meant for you is a sweet revelation. It is kindly noted that, hurt people, hurt people and defeat people, defeat people. Our purity is worth more than those who are a conflict of interest to our peace and purpose (2 Corinthians 6:14-18 NKJV). Our space requires change, a pure alignment with our Heavenly Creator. And if you are the hurt and defeated people, seek God and trust His therapeutical strategies.

We must effectively understand our alignment with God, "we need to understand condemnation" (Montgomery, T. 2020). Our position is within God; our brand is within God, our purpose with God (Anthony, S. 2020). God made His dwelling place within us, right here with us. May we allow God who is within to activate His Spirit and penetrate without?

> But blessed is the man who trusts me, God, the woman who sticks with God. They're like trees replanted in Eden, putting down roots near the rivers — Never a worry through the hottest of summers, never dropping a leaf, Serene and calm through droughts, bearing fresh fruit every season. (Jer. 17:7-8 MSG)

"Fasting and praying are powerful spiritual tools" that will also help us to discern our purpose (Montgomery, 2020). God is a confirming and assuring God as He truly cares to direct our paths as we acknowledge Him in every single way; fasting and praying our next level ways of acknowledgement (Prov.s 3:6 NKJV). In receiving every good and perfect gift from above, preparation ensures a sound mind (James 1:17 KJV).

> For God hath not given us the spirit of fear; but of power, and of love, and of a sound mind. (2 Tim. 1:7 KJV)

God calls us to solely rely on Hm. All the glory belongs to God as shared in Chapter 1 *Falling in Love with God* and Chapter 6 *Focus*, as we do not live by bread alone. Hope is also a powerful complementing spiritual strength that is purely developed as we exercise our prayer muscles and trust God's supernatural will. Christ sacrificed His life for us, and simple, pure courtesy is to sacrifice our life (time, energy, efforts) for Him. May we not lose sight of glorifying and honoring God for our purpose in Him? There is something beautiful inside of us that is in need of blooming outside of us into the world, that only God has the power to release. Our purpose lies within the eye of our beholder.

Faith

Building faith is becoming triumphant. Our God is faithful to those faithful to Him. Don't we all desire faithfulness, trustworthiness, commitment? *Don't* we all desire a relationship filled with everlasting peace and love. *Don't* we all desire joy? Well, where do we believe this desire comes from? We can only wonder for so long until we truly encounter the goodness of our Lord and savior. We triumphantly execute and conquer our purpose as we walk with God, by faith. God only understands and operates on faith, as should we. God is faithful, trustworthy, and committed to securing our peace, love, joy.

Life becomes more fun and adventurous as we build our faith in our God almighty. As opposed to leading our own lives, faith welcomes God to lead us into purity. Given that we tend to be unfaithful with ourselves, which trigger unwise decisions, we delegate the authority from self to God. We welcome a new GPS operation better known as God Protects Souls.

May our newly found GPS become the best friend we never had, the right hand we have ever longed for, the jelly to our peanut butter, the chocolate chips to our chocolate ice cream, the cream to our cheese, the shake to our milk (and that is non dairy of course). May God become the pure peace, love, joy our soul has awaited since our birth? God was, is, and will forever be God. God created us in pure love and protected us for this moment of time. God is in the business of protecting souls. Activating this protection is our map to His promised land. Successfully activating this GPS will provide purity and clarity.

As we faithfully trust God's divine purpose for our life, the sweeter each day will be. God also assures us that faith without works is dead (James 2:26 KJV). Therefore we believe in faith as well as pursue in faith. Our purpose was especially created by His power and authority. There is a healthy level of being still, and having faith that God's power reigns while striving faithfully on His strength in obedience, Establishing and fulfilling our purpose requires our being deeply rooted in faith as opposed to being tossed to and fro.

We are strong. We can do ALL things through Christ who strengthens us (Phil. 4:13 KJV). Believe this, wholeheartedly. He will never leave us nor forsake us as we embrace His way (I Kings 8:57 KJV). His way is our purity. His way is our peace. His way is our strength. God's love is an experience like no other.

Shine

Jewel, precious, Jewel, shine honey, shine. Shine, shine, shine. The world awaits our precious, bright light of goodness. We owe the world truth. We owe God our heart of purity. Our lives are precious. God graced us with the breath of life as well as power and authority. To shine is to win. To win is to grind. Moving, grinding, living, and loving with pure motives is a breath of fresh air. Setting and achieving goals is too a healthy practice when done with a pure conscience.

In shining righteously, we are to be intentional in being better. We are to be intentional in living on God's purpose. Living in purpose manifests one's fulfillment. While setting goals and intentionally creating a lifestyle to achieve them is God's plan. To shine also requires discipline and commitment. Practical measures include spending time assessing, understanding, organizing spiritual goals. For instance, prioritizing our spiritual well being and deciding, what biblical character will we strive to be like this month? Which biblical character will we aim to learn more about? What aspect of our character will we focus on developing? In which ways will we surrender our time to God to hear His voice? When will we surrender our business to God, allowing Him his rightful CEO role? When will we invest in a prayer journal to write our love letters to God? When will we seek clarification on how to shine brighter in our purpose?

We experience pure goodness in life as we focus on growth. May we never stop growing, never stop glowing. May our lights of righteousness never dim? May our lights brighten up nations (Gen. 12:2 NKJV). May we never stop leveling up with Christ? We experience pure goodness in life as we focus on growth. Let's embrace all the beauty there is in life by focusing on leveling up, growing.

Discipline and commitment is required to level up and strengthen our mind. A healthy lifestyle requires a wholeness approach. We can only truly embrace our spiritual health given our discipline in praying, fasting, communing, and reading God's word of strategy. Our physical, nutritional, and emotional (mental) health are also important; cherishing the life God gifted us. Fully embracing our physical health consists of regular exercising, while our nutritional health consists of eating well.

Taking care of our body is an honorable commitment that we truly understand as we reverence God for creating us. Gifts are valuable and sentimental, as well as forever cherished. Our emotional health is a direct replica of our spiritual health. With this being said prayer and praise to prepare us to shine. We are beautiful. We are special. We are talented. We are gifted; we are a gift. May we be the ray of sunshine that we are destined to be. May we be healthy, be free.

Strength

> Your righteousness, oh God, which is the high heavens. You who have done great things, oh God, who is like you? You have made me see many troubles and calamities will revive me again; from the depths of the earth you will bring me up again. You will increase my greatness and comfort me again. (Ps. 71:19-21 ESV)

God's love ignites our emotional health. We are emotionally and mentally equipped as we are spiritually fuelled. The strength of our emotional health requires a strong spiritual health. Strength is formed in the depths of pure roots within our soul. Inner peace is a pure reflection of spiritual ground. Outer strength is a pure reflection of our spiritual growth.

The stature of our heart is more valuable than the stature of our deed (Jer. 17:10 NKJV). God reveals what is not clean in order to make us clean. If our soul is off, our emotions will always be off, fluctuating with no stability. As we propel spiritually, we also propel emotionally, as well as mentally, physically, socially, financially.

God is our teacher of strength. And a student of great form brings great results. Spiritual form begins with our heart posture, which is complimented by daily devotion to read His word, hear His voice, and execute His will. Reflecting on our current way of life will allow us to change and become amazing students. Our overflow of peace and love stems from our heart posture, not the size of our booty or amount of people we have sex with.

There are many situations in life that have deeply affected our mind resulting in a hindrance to our emotional and spiritual health. God has a way of gracefully convicting, healing, and strengthening us. Being gracefully broken becomes a perfect testimony with God's deliverance (Rev. 12:11 KJV).

Testimonies are our strength, and a way to shine and we save the loss with our empowering story. And through this brokenness God produces greatness. When we are weak He makes us strong; in our perfect weakness God makes us perfectly powerful (2 Cor. 12:9 NKJV).

Yet in all these things we are more than conquerors through Him who loved us. (Rom. 8:37 NKJV)

Because of Jesus, we are strong. Because of Jesus our strength is on *fleek, fleek*! Discovering purpose, discovering wholeness is an individual process. When dating, prayer, praise, and worship is uplifting to God, though building a personal relationship with our Heavenly Father will benefit your dating relationship, marriage God willing, and ultimately you.

Worshipping, praising, honoring, and glorifying God enables a supernatural strength and encounter of His heavenly realm. Pure love and strength is nurtured by God's goodness. God shines on us as we worship in spirit, worship in truth. God shines on us as we walk in favor and joy.

God has a special will for us where we shine as we embrace all of His goodness and trust His strategic path.

May we discover the peace within us, discover the strength within us. May we discover the light we truly are. May we discover how to love purely, how to love righteously, how to love selflessly, how to love humbly. May we discover growth in our heavenly Father, how to strengthen our strengths, how to improve our weaknesses. May we discover commitment, and how to focus on blooming, blossoming. May we reflect and discover how to become whole.

The world is full of goodness. We are full of goodness. "The world is waiting to see the God you serve through the work you do. People are waiting to see the manifestation through your life given the power of the God you serve, which you honor adore" (Montgomery, 2020). There's so much beauty to appreciate and produce.

Our mentality is valuable when fueled with goodness though invaluable when not fueled with goodness. May we live purely, joyfully, wonderfully, righteously, selflessly, lovingly, confidently, and faithfully. May we embrace life to the absolute fullest. Reflecting and deflecting provides opportunity to grow. Renewing, rebuilding, restoring are equally helpful tools to develop your mind and embrace your soul. Many things shape our views; however, God's view is the absolute purest. And we only truly appreciate that life is beautiful as we reflect, knowing that strength is but a breath away.

Reflection

- How will you begin to build your faith?
- How will you begin to change to pursue your God given purpose?

- How are you intentionally fulfilling your life's purpose today? Pause, think, write.
- Read Psalm 29
- Read Matthew 3
- Read Ephesians 4

11

REJUVENATE

Do you ever think about death? Do you ever think about exiting the world, parting from family, separating from assets? What are your thoughts about death? What are your thoughts about eternity? Do you understand there is life after death? Do you understand that you can experience more life here on earth, more peace, love, and joy? Have you imagined being even more alive, a sense of pure rejuvenation? Have you imagined pure freedom, to live pure, free of sexual immortality, pornography, abuse, masturbation, fornication, emotional dramas, and emotional rollercoasters?

The definition of rejuvenate is to make someone or something look or feel more refresher, younger, and lively. God is our rejuvenator. Other words that describe rejuvenate are revive, renew, restore. In God we are revived, renewed, restored from all emotional traumas, heartbreaks, losses. Restoration is an extremely important experience in building a strong foundation and relationship with our heavenly Father.

God cares to restore us to experience His power, might, and most intimately His spirit. God cares to restore us because neglect was never His will. Emptiness is a means of the enemy as he too is empty and eternally defeated. Remember, misery loves company as well as hurt people hurt people, and defeated people defeat people. Well those people are battling with God's enemy, Satan.

We are deeply in need of restoration because we have developed an impure lifestyle, jeopardizing our blessings from God. At times we are naive or oblivious to the fact that we are being emptied, slowly but surely. As we reflect, we actually will identify the roots of certain trends that lead to our emptied parts. In healing emotionally, we spiritually need to take time, be still, and reflect. In these moments we choose to learn life, learn God. Rejuvenation is living truth. In order to trail blaze in our purpose, the effective measures of healing our wounds firstly are to renounce their impact. And secondly is to allow God to rejuvenate our hearts and replenish our souls of pure love, joy, peace within.

True rejuvenation is the awe and fullness of hugs, kisses, and blessings poured in our life by the strength of faith. Rejuvenation occurs as we allow for God to fulfill His purposeful role within our life. Rejuvenation is also factored with forgiveness as we read in Chapter 3, Protecting Our Jewels. The significant factor is that the purpose of forgiveness is for rebuilding self. While, establishing pure standards will enable us to grow amazingly. We learn to have a forgiving heart as God. There is redundancy in aiming for rejuvenation if we have not forgiven ourselves or others, of the life we are parting with.

Prayer guidance and proper restorative wellbeing as mentioned in Chapter 2 and 5 will assist us in a smooth rejuvenation process. Growth is a daily exercise, complimented with rejuvenation in God's word, and repentance. Our emotions are stable with a strong Godly spirit. "Restoration is God rejuvenating us as if the past never happened or occurred" (Lyles, 2020). Prayer is a gateway to experiencing His restoration. Restoration is a form of God's grace elevating us to where we were meant to be hadn't we been distracted. Worldly progression such as titles and things has nothing on restoration, Godly elevation.

Be Woke, Stay Woke

Why not go above and beyond to be better? Why not focus on our spiritual health in order to strengthen our emotional health? Why not try God and be relieved of pain? Why not reset, refocus on being healthy all-round, one day at a time? Let's invest more time in our personal well being than in the latest media report, twitter post, group chat. We become woke with God, let's stay woke. When we are healthy, we become wealthy.

Wealth is an abundance of valuable possessions, plentiful supplies of a particular resource. God is our wealth. We become woke and wealthy as we rejuvenate with our heavenly Father. We also have the beautiful burning flame within that we accidently desire to explode without, sharing God's good news, and as such, the birth of Jewel, Precious Jewel. God instills a luxury of wealth to inspire and help others to be healthy, be fruitful. We need God to enhance our spiritual health in order to address the other aspects of health.

The different forms of health complement each other. Without one or the other is like trying to drive a car on "Empty" and without the key (because it has been misplaced). Well there the issue lies, we need gas to fuel the car and the key to start the ignition right? In life, we need God, Jesus Christ, and His Holy Spirit to thrive. We need to eat well and exercise well to survive. A relationship with our heavenly Father will set the preliminaries to manage our emotions. We need His power and authority above all to conquer all things and achieve wholeness.

The reality is we have been more consumed with intoxicating our minds, bodies, souls and are slowly dying a quick death when God is absent from our lives. What does a slow, quick death mean? Well, there is righteousness and evilness. Our God is righteous while our enemy is evil. There is also a heavenly realm filled with all of God's goodness and an enemy realm filled with evilness. In the heavenly realm is God's Kingdom of Heaven which naturally thrives and flourishes in pure, perfect peace and love.

In alluding to the reality of a slow, quick, death we are living in a spiritual warfare. We are familiar with the sayings, good over evil or good over bad, there is no in between. Our mighty God has actually pre-warned us of this concept in advance with His holy word. Unfortunately, we have tendencies to adopt things of the world as opposed to things of heaven; the world has been intoxicated with evil and impurity. God says we are either for Him or against Him (Matt. 12:30 NKJV).

We either choose to live faithfully with Him or unfaithfully without Him. Living unfaithfully without God is a battle of control, greed, and or wrath. Without God, motives are skewed. It's almost as if sin is so addictive and appears to be appealing in the moment but in actuality is causing depletion within our cells and a form of numbness to righteousness. Therefore, a sinful lifestyle causes a lingering of demonic spirits to infiltrate among our relationships, our choices, and our finances to name a few (1 Jhn 3:8 NKJV).

Many times the demonic spirits are not vividly recognizable; they can be misleading though *pleasing*. The book cover of sins requires spiritual discernment and righteous judgment. Some of us are in sexual relationships, and our partners are abusive emotionally, mentally, and or physically. The very saddening and disturbing fact is that these relationships may *feel* right or normal; this has become our set norm.

Some of us are in sexual relationships, and we are extremely discontent, dissatisfied, and deeply unhappy with ourselves. We believe that we are not worthy; because of our lack of security and confidence we cling towards relationships that distract us from addressing our true needs. While some of us have developed multiple sexual relationships over time. We have neither paused nor reflected on how to live differently. Because having multiple partners has been our reality we tend to believe that is our self value. Yet we are sleeping on our own potential, our true worth.

Without restoration, given these scenarios, we have likely died already giving the enemy the upper hand of our lives. We have likely *died* internally because we have given up on believing there is a better alternative or accepting these rooted impurities to rule over our life. The roots of insecurities, abortions, abuse, and unhealthy (toxic) relationships are so deep that we either immune to this way of life or have invested majority of our life drowning in toxic relationships. Yet our God rescues and saves us from sinking and losing our last bit of oxygen.

There is a lack of clarity and certainty because purity has not been our priority. Go figure, purity is not *typically* "sexy." And in this case sexy refers to being glorified or glamoured. Being pure is not praised because why? Modesty isn't sellable? Honesty isn't attainable? When living faithfully to and consciously of God, Jesus Christ, and the Holy Spirit, purity is a natural focus. The trinity is our true and actual power force, our clarity and our certainty.

Praise

Praise be to God forever and ever, amen. Praise be to God in the highest, heavenly realm. Praise be to God who created heaven and earth. Praise be to God who created our intricate parts, and designed an intimate exchange of prayer and praise. Praise, honor, power be to God for His perfection. Adoration be to God for choosing us to rise today with breath and life.

Adoration be to God for saving us from our shortcomings, bringing us high when we were low. Glory be to God for the time that is now, reading and learning more about His power in making us new, purifying our lives. Glory be to God for renewing our minds, rejuvenating our body, restoring our souls.

> Glory to God in the highest, and on earth peace, good will toward men. (Lk. 2:14 KJV)

> Praise God in heaven! Peace on earth to everyone who pleases God. (Lk. 2:14 CEV)

Praise is pure focus on every single good and perfect aspect of life. Praise is pure honor to our heavenly Father for our precious gift of life. Praise is pure glory and power to God for pure freedom within His holy presence. Praise is choosing to count it all joy. Praise is appreciating each lesson that has occurred to make us better, acknowledging each setback as the best experiential come back, reflecting on each trial as a means to become stronger. As we praise, we rejuvenate. As we praise, we replenish. God has an intimate, special divine love that fills us. A love and peace that fills us up, all the way up.

God is in control. The sooner we fully honor, respect, and appreciate His pure authority, the sooner we fully experience pure freedom. With God we are free of fear. With God we become pure, purely whole. Lessons, setbacks, and trials happen for reasons beyond our control. And as a matter of fact, life is beyond our control. However, we have security and confidence in God, who is in control. We praise God for revelations and strategies to prepare, progress as well as succeed. We praise God because His divine control, knowing that He who began a good work within us would bring it to completion, and rejuvenate us all throughout our journey.

To love God is a choice and experience. The choice of acknowledging His creation and those we too are a part of His wondrous works begins deep down in our heart. The emotion is strong, and the sentiment is real. The choice of accepting Jesus Christ in our life and allowing Him to be the Lord over our lives changes the dynamic of our life. We no longer cater to our sinful desires but cater to those of God, which is so rejuvenating. We earnestly seek to glorify, honor, and praise God with our entire being. We no longer chose to be enslaved to sin but be servants of God's righteous kingdom. We understand that life has pure purpose when we fulfill the path of our creator's divine design intended for us.

Honoring God is another way to acknowledge and commune with Him. Acknowledging God for our gift of life is a joy we should be forever grateful for. Thinking of giving respect, where respect is due, God deserves all honor, praise, and respect. His creation is our playground; He is our freedom, and our home. With God we have freedom presently and eternally. Honoring God is a privilege. While on earth we are privileged to experience the adventures of faith building, hearing His voice, and building His Kingdom.

Worship

God is perfect. God is power. God is love. God is pure. God is grace. God is peace. God is love. God is health. God is wealth. God is joy. God is victory. God is precious. God is honor. God is great. God is grace. God is mercy. God is perfect, yes perfect. And unsurprisingly the perfection of God is mentioned over three-hundred times in Jewel. God created us perfect before we became imperfect. Worship God, praise God, honor God, glorify God. Worship is rejuvenating.

Pure love is nurtured by God's goodness. We worship because of God's goodness and instantly experience peace, instantly experience love. There is power in God's peace. And as we worship, as we honor God with our heart, mind, soul, strength, body, we receive all His goodness. God has no time for impure games. God knows our heart. Shall we not be in it to win it with God, we hinder our worship.

Praise and worship are pure loving measures of our expression to God. God is synced with praise and worship which brings pure joy to His ears. God is naturally aligned with worship which is another delightful love language of His. Along with God communicating with us in various ways such as dreams, we have freedom to communicate with God through prayer (thanksgiving), praise (rejoice), and worship (honor). God loves as we pray, commune, praise, and worship His Holy name. Each is equally God's love language.

Having bold faith is admirable. Having strong faith is admirable. Having an attractive faith is admirable. Confidence and assurance is our standard of worship. We confidently worship our victory in Him. We celebrate our newness and freshness in God. We celebrate our stable emotions. We celebrate our rise in God's glory, unashamed, unbothered, and unhurt. We celebrate our season of purity. Our heads are expected to be held high in worship as God is our peace, and has given us pure peace.

God is in pure awe as we worship, praise, honor, and glorify his Holy name. The King of Kings, Lord of Lords, our mighty God oh how He loves us. God loves us unconditionally. God desires us to experience heaven on earth. We experience joy, peace, love as we celebrate the pure harmony with God's perfection, goodness, grace, mercy. God is perfect.

God created us perfectly, purposefully to sing, praise, and worship gloriously. Our worship is a part of our rejuvenation.

Our heart is the most severely, delicate part of our being, spiritually as well as physically. Our heart is also the most vital organ within the body, a divine design of God's intricate orchestrations. God perfectly orchestrated our heart as the most vital organ as a central positioning of His pure love. Our heart gives the body life. Our heart gives the body hope. Our heart gives the body function. Our heart gives the body purpose. This organ is vital being the core part of our body, the core reason allowing life to be. Spiritually, the heart allows for God's gifts to flow and glow. Physically, the heart allows for blood flow and oxygen to travel through our body, to and from this organ.

Worship begins in our heart. We worship because of God. We have life because of God. We honor God with a heart of worship. The delicacy of our heart is direct intimacy with God's Holy Spirit. Our sensitivity to God's spirit is rooted within our heart. As God's word flows through our heart, He manifests and produces His spiritual intents (Hew. 4:12 KJV). God's spiritual fruits naturally (freely) flow from us as our heart consumes His word and follows His spirit's lead. Being sensitive to His spirit allows us to confidently walk in His spirit realm and hear God's voice. Trust and faith is built as His spirit perfectly guides us through every move. We exercise our spirit with reading, praying, fasting, praising, worshipping. We become spiritually fit as we condition our heart with regular worship. Implementing worship in our lifestyle is spiritually necessary to strengthen our heart's muscle.

Equally to exercising with physical weights, gym machines (equipment), or body conditional movements allowing the external body to become healthy, we exercise the internal body to become healthy. Physically, our external body requires consistent weight training and stretching. Our muscles are ripped as we lift and strengthened as we stretch. The pain is real and we focus on becoming strong as pain leaves the body. The health of our heart also is supported by our cardiovascular movement, improving blood flow. Spiritually our internal body requires consistent worship training, to allow God's peace to flow. God is our coach, trainer, cheerleader, all while equipping us for His great work. God's word encourages us that our race is not a sprint, yet a marathon. Training this course demands are mind to be focused, body to be fit, spirit to be hydrated.

May we each meditate on and eat His Holy word daily. May we each sing gladly with pure minds, bodies (hearts), souls. May we each praise and worship God's sweet, sweet perfect name. Reading our Heavenly Creator's word does the soul oh so good. The Bible is the best daily bread we can ever consume, having the perfect sweet and spice. This precious book is the most perfect nourishment and nutrition. Oh the joys of reading God's word, building faith, worshipping His Holy name, becoming whole is the greatest rewarding, fulfilling experience.

Grow

God is all about levels. There is a wealth of knowledge to gain from God, our Father. God expects us to level up in His spiritual realm. Knowledge is deliverance (Osei, 2020). God expects us to grow more pure each day. Growth becomes our new norm and an exciting thrill when we honor God to be the Lord over our life.

As we grow with God, we only long to shine, grow, and be better. Being better is in actuality being more like Christ. Leveling up requires a humble attitude towards growth, accepting that there is always room to grow, always. God needs us to also have a heart conditioned to pruning and leveling up. There is no particular manual in what we need to grow in today or tomorrow, though there will always be a character trait, thought process, or heart condition in need of alignment with Christ.

Jesus is the *big brother* we never had from the perspective of God being our heavenly father. Jesus, in fact is our earthly representation of God.Jesus is the only idol we too should ever have, he is God. As we acknowledge Jesus for His perfection we understand that He is too our God (in the flesh, and commonly known as the son of God). Jesus Christ is the perfect example to admire. He is the recipe to our growth.

God's intention for growth is twofold. In one aspect we grow sensitive to God's word, way, will and focus on being better, more like Christ. As we embrace the *aha* moment that God is in fact God, that we are because God is. We naturally desire to know more and be more. It's exactly like the time a child discovers to crawl, and then realizes they could walk, and then run. These transitions were neither smooth (or without correction), we sometimes cried our hearts out, injured our knees, or tripped over our ankles. In reality, God needs to prune us as we journey through our process of growth. And in order to embrace His correction, we are to surrender and submit.

> When I was a child, I spoke as a child, I understood as a child, I thought as a child; but when I became a man, I put away childish things. (1 Cor. 13:11 NKJV)

Imagine the first plane ride, when we realized we can in fact fly. We no longer crawl because of growth and maturity. We understand that there are greater, higher advantages to running. We understand the importance of correction. We understand there is more to discover as we level up. We understand that as a child we could only consume soft foods, then as an adult we could now consume solids. Spiritually, God is our solid food, our greatest *grease*. Spiritually, as we level up God calls us to run with Him, soar (fly high) with Him, while consuming all His goodness.

To grow is specifically designed for the purpose of leveling up, as we master one level, we grow on to the next. Once we humble our heart and purify our spirit, we only desire to fly high with God. We are meant to fly. God calls us to fly and build His kingdom, humbly so. God is too great to have us crawling around trying to walk into our purpose. As we level up, we are to forever honor His Holy name, remembering He who forgives us, teaches us, blesses us, while equips us to grow in order to have a prosperous hope and a future.

> For I know the plans I have for you," declares the LORD, "plans to prosper you and not to harm you, plans to give you hope and a future. (Jer. 29:11 NIV)

We will forever be an actual child before God. Growth is to understand that we will always be children of God; as a child needs nurture, guidance, direction, correction, so do we. God, our heavenly Father longs to hold us dear. Our heart is in need of consistent love and discipline. Our heavenly Father is the only being able to assess and correct our heart posture. Growth is also willing to be corrected regularly.

God has given each and every one of us a choice, however we commonly choose the opposite to righteousness. Therefore we are living according to the enemy's plagues and are slowly being victimized by his destruction. God assures us that we must worship the Lord our God, and serve Him only (Lk. 4:3-4 NKJV). We can only get to the place God has called us to be by , fulfilling our destiny as we grow. And the way we grow is to learn, understand God's will for our life. Our responsibility is serving the Lord, and growing whilst we serve in all humillity. We have to master God's level of growth in order to understand that humility is actually being an "adult" child.

May our lives always become better and not be the same as in our youth. May we not only grow physically, but mentally and spiritually. May we do what is conducive to the heart of God. May we always be like a child before God. May our transformation be evident and cause others to draw nearer to God. May we testify that only God's word truly transforms us. May we explain the great news of Jesus Christ, rejuvenation, growth. May we hear God, and allow Him to speak to our mind, body, soul, spirit. May we hear and obey immediately, confidently as the Lord calls us.

God is an honorable and integral father. A woman of God recently shared that there is a society that operates as visitors to heaven's door. We become a part of God's Kingdom as we live for Him. Growth is a permanent status not a visitor's status. To live a lukewarm lifestyle is unruly yet unnecessary. Again, only communicating with a friend because we need a favor demonstrates a lack of appreciation. By no means does our heavenly father stand and operate in a lukewarm manner. His commands and orders for our life to be filled with rejuvenation are simple and clear. God is our rejuvenator, reviver, and restorer.

Growth is embracing all the beauty around us, within us. Growth is embracing the gifts we were graciously blessed with. Growth is embracing new beginnings and new opportunities to be better, to be greater. Growth is embracing new ideas, new opportunities, new investments, new seasons, new perspectives, new mentalities, new strategies, and new lifestyles. Growth is embracing a lifestyle that is truly uplifting and fulfilling. True fulfillment endures strength when the world may be weak. True fulfillment experiences peace when the world may worry. True peace, strength, growth is favored and graced by God.

Being still yet being wise is nurtured by growth. When we are still we appreciate all the goodness around us and embrace new revelation in managing our health, physically, spiritually, nutritionally, emotionally. Let's embrace the beauty that surrounds us and let's focus on the perfection of God's natural gifts. We are created for more, more peace, strength, and opportunity to grow.

Reflection

- What in your life needs to be purged and uprooted to embrace your optimal life?
- How are you living today to please our heavenly father? What can you do differently to fulfill a more pure, healthy, joyful lifestyle?
- How are you drawing closer to our heavenly father when in need of rejuvenation?
- How are you rejuvenating and becoming more pure?
- How is praise and worship a form of rejuvenation?
- How are you spending your days renewing your mind, rebuilding your body strength, restoring your soul?
- What actions can you implement to have a more rejuvenating life?

12

TRAILBLAZE

He who says he abides in Him ought himself also to walk just as He walked. **1 John 2:6 (NKJV)**

Living for God is the purest experience we'll ever encounter. In living for God we understand the value of purity. We understand that God is pure and solemnly desires us to be pure. In becoming pure, growing and living for God there is a level of grit to endure. We are to fight this good fight knowing that trouble may come our way, weapons may form against us, but the power of God within us will forever trail blaze.

Fighting God's good fight is the best battle to pursue. Fighting to win God's glory has everlasting rewards. What's better than everlasting victory? Yes, exactly, nothing. Fighting to win God's glory includes trailblazing through temptation, rejection, and confrontation (Jhn. 14:12 NKJV). When sexual, sinful desires approach, we prevail with God.

To prevail is defined as to prove more powerful than opposing forces; be victorious. We are more powerful than temptations. We are more powerful than rejections. We are more powerful than confrontations. We need only to utilize our power force, God. His strategy and strength allows us to power through opposition. As we think about or desire to have sex, we pray. As we fantasize about sex and we are married, we pray. As we lustfully admire photos or people before us, we pray. To understand our power and authority is praying God's word, commending that He transforms us by the renewing of our mind in Jesus' mighty name (Rom. 12:2 NKJV).

Shouts of joy, we sing songs of deliverance in these very moments. Our shouts deliver us to prevail. God exceeds our expectation and changes our heart as we pursue purity. We are not to be cut short on our assignment for God. Some of us have been mindlessly living; we have become either too complacent or nonchalant. We have business matters to tend to, great, executive missions to complete. Increasing our sex partner count is taking us further away from what's really good. Having the most revealing Instagram photo is damaging our mind from what's really good. Seeking to alter God's perfect creation is diminishing our body. Aiming to settle in a relationship for the sake of status is ruining our spirit.

Sexual desires are one of our greatest physical impurities. Meanwhile, sexual desires lead to conflict and confusion. As a result of God's absence, there is an absence of structure and standard. Instability occurs because our flesh is weak. Shall we have struggles of cheating, lying, miscommunication; these factors will too affect our relationships. And in other news, the age range worldwide of our first sexual encounter is between seventeen and twenty-four.

Perhaps some of us were younger or older, or anticipate(d) on being older people, this is a general statistic. Either way, this means that we have a lot of sex before even becoming secure in our self. We have a lot of sex before even understanding our purpose, let alone living within our purpose. We have a lot of sex before even grasping the depths of trailblazing victoriously because our level of thinking is narrow. We have been influenced by emotions that we believed only sex can address. So to prevail through these desires may seem far fetched. This is because of our slim thoughts and experience of the magnitude of God.

When friendships dwindle, we rise with God. When past affairs resurface, we arise with God. Worship trembles the Satan who is the ring leader of sin. As we worship and pray, God's angels tend to our every need. Sexual desires are sinful spirits that aim to hold us hostage. Rejection and confrontation are also tactics of the enemy to emotionally and mentally defeat us. However, we are trailblazers in it to win it.

> The Lord gives voice before His army, For His camp is very great; For strong is the One who executes His word. For the day of the Lord is great and very terrible; Who can endure it? (Jl 2:11 NKJV)

We are to conquer all odds, overcome all battles, win all fights righteously so. Although we may have been defeated, we have victory in God. Although we may have been discouraged, we are encouraged with God. Victory is in the eye of a champion. We are champions, champions of purity as we trail blaze through temptation. Our sinful desires end now, because we are trailblazers and fighters for God. Our focus is God, our focus is purity.

In leveling up and achieving more, we have to believe that we too are conquerors. We have to be willing to go above and beyond. We have to be willing to level up. We have to be willing to be made well. We have to be willing to always elevate. We have to be willing to be better, the best version of ourselves. We must seek change in order to change. How hungry are you to prepare for each new level God has for you?

Then Jesus turned to the Jews who had claimed to believe in him. "If you stick with this, living out what I tell you, you are my disciples for sure. Then you will experience for yourselves the truth, and the truth will free you. (Jhn. 8:31-32 MSG)

The truth sets us free. Jesus' nature among earth was clear, direct, and simple. No matter which angle we decide to presume and or justify the life we live, there is and will forever be one truth. The truth simply requires our acceptance. For what we know and choose not to abide is sin against God. And what we do not know is for lack of wisdom. "But when we resist or disavow knowledge, when we profess ignorance as a way of donning armor and evading accountability, then we make a mockery of those words, and we rupture connections not only with others but within ourselves, within our souls" (Cohen, L. H., 2013).

God loves us too, too much not to allow us to be a trailblazer for His glory. He is constantly revealing Himself in our lives going to and fro, remember (2 Chr. 16:9 NKJV), awaiting our acknowledgement. And as we acknowledge that He is Lord, we humbly repent, and lovingly follow His lead. Chapter 9 has addressed God going to and fro to assess our hearts post our commitment to Him; He also has awaited our hearts prior to our commitment. The truth is, God loves us and will forever love us, the question is, will we love Him back? Will we trail blaze for His love? When we experience God, we experience truth. Ultimately we experience freedom, the epitome of peace and purity in which we would have it no other way.

The truth is plain and simple. Focusing on God, and abiding in God (His word) is pure discipline. Relationships require discipline and commitment. However our journey with Christ, our loving God is the most important one. Our journey towards heaven is the sweetest bliss as we trail blaze righteously.

May we not go back, yet always strive to go ahead. God desires us to progress and go forward with Him. Jewel was written as a tool to support our journey of purity. This book was written to help set us free. This book was written to guide us on how to thrive with God, purely. Because we have made it this far, we have no right but to trailblazers through our current fires and or any forest to come. Trailblazing may be difficult but with God it is made easy. Trailblazing may be tiring but with God we have rest. (1 King 5:4 KJV)

Prepare

Prepare for a lifestyle that is forever teaching, blooming, trailblazing. Prepare to always be excited by God's revelations. Prepare to always embrace more of God. Prepare to always glorify God. Prepare to save souls. Prepare to be purer each day. Prepare to purify your mind, body, soul, spirit and trailblaze like no tomorrow. Prepare to be gifted by the gifts of God's spirit.

We are to develop security and wisdom in Christ Jesus our Lord. Preparing to live for His righteousness, prepares us to be living testimonies in glorifying His kingdom. We were created and designed to live for His glory, to experience His glory, though we have been playing. We must admit that we have been playing foolish games. Our lack of fulfillment is due to our lack of preparedness and sinfulness. God does not know lack, He represents fullness, wholeness. His kingdom is filled with goodness and abundance of wealth. God's wealth is peace, love, joy, contentment. Like every experience of value, we have to prepare. Our final test is obtaining the salvation which is in Christ Jesus (2 Timothy 2:10 KJV) .

We are to be prepared to pass God's test, the realest test of our lifetime. And, yes the sweetest journey as we prepare to die to our sinful ways and live God's way.

God desires us to arise and shine, our time is now. The only games we should be playing are the ones that involve winning the prize of purity and victory. Let's be prepared, let's be proactive. Being prepared stems from confirming our focus. As we determine our focus we prepare and strategize ways to faithfully believe and achieve greatness. Reading Jewel, our focus originally was our determination of becoming pure and understanding the process of achieving purity. Although purity is not a game, we shall testify and celebrate achievements of abstinence (weekly, monthly, yearly), cleanliness (changed, environments, friendships, consumptions), and focus.

God will turn our current story to His story allowing for nations to be blessed and influenced. We are influencers. We are producers. We are trailblazers. Our focus of becoming pure before God is worthy to be praised. God is worthy to be praised as He infiltrates our toxins and replenishes our souls. He prepares us each day as we read His word, pray His word, and desire His will. (Psalms 23:5 NKJV) His signs, wonders, and miracles appear everywhere. The thought of sexual immorality and the smell of alcohol disgust us after God deals with us, lovingly so. As only He could purify us, the testimonies are victories. God prepares us spiritually, as we choose to be prepared mentally.

God has already prepared us for a great work shall we honor our perfect purpose in Him. In God we are prepared to achieve all things great, in alignment to His will. In God we are prepared to be made new, whole, and pure. We are further prepared for greatness in Christ as we pray, fast, and tithe. As we pray we acknowledge God's truth. As we fast we discern God's voice. And as we tithe we build our faith in God we trust.

Tithe

> For even during a season of severe difficulty and tremendous suffering, they became even more filled with joy. From the depths of their extreme poverty, super-abundant joy overflowed into an act of extravagant generosity. For I can verify that they spontaneously gave, not only according to their means but far beyond what they could afford. (2 Cor. 8:2-3 TPT)

We are God's ambassadors. In order for His purpose to be fulfilled in our lives, tithing is a spiritual principle of strengthening our trust with Him. The first percent of our earnings is entitled to be returned in faith to God for the development of His Kingdom. Our lives, our families, our businesses, our money sincerely belongs to Him. As we entrust in pure faith our earnings to God, He recognizes our obedience and maturity while increasing our load on earth. God trusts those who rely on Him, because He is all knowing. We must seek His spiritual moves in order to succeed and trail blaze in everything we do.

God is a perfect multiplier. As He recognizes our sacrifice, He multiplies our favor. Our sacrifice can also be to condemn our old way of living. Sins that may have been pleasing to our flesh, a part of our sinful nature become a sacrifice as we choose God's greater good. God increases our wisdom as we devote to Him. God also strengthens and enhances our life as we devote our earnings back to Him. Recognizing that we are blessed and favored because of God's provision, we are tested to respond with thanksgiving in this manner. As we tithe God naturally multiplies the giving for a greater testimony. We sacrifice our time, learning His word, discerning His voice, praying for His spiritual direction. We sacrifice our money investing in purposeful ministries that help to plant seeds of righteousness for God's glory, sharing and preaching His Holy word among the nations. God sacrificed His first and only son to give us salvation, imagine the overflow of blessings to manifest from following His lead.

Tithing is faith led. We tithe into our future. The more we surrender, and entrust God with what the world believes most valuable, we gain one hundred folds from our giving. The purpose of our giving is to financially pour into God's Kingdom and physically establish ministries.God's ministries are also proposed to trail blaze. God's Kingdom is community, the community that becomes family, helps to create brotherly love lead proper prayer and teach His word. Tithing is another trust factor in which God tests and assesses our heart to determine what is really good, *what time it is*. We reap what we sow is directly from the principals of God himself. The more we hear, trust, and obey, the more we receive. One of God's purposes for tithing and simply His way of doing is that we fully submit to His control in all humility. And to credit Him, we continue to praise, worship, praise some more, pray, build, and tithe. Imagine the relationships and businesses to come from God. Imagine the strength and security to develop from God. We tithe with purpose; we tithe with a pure heart because God says so.

> For you have experienced the extravagant grace of our Lord Jesus Christ, that although he was infinitely rich, he impoverished himself for our sake, so that by his poverty, we could become rich beyond measure. (2 Cor. 8:9 TPT)

We need the most serious stripping of all time. We have become strapped with and entangled in sin. Specifically speaking of sex, we have adopted this entitlement that we are owed something for nothing. We tend to expect to receive free exchanges. Yes, God's love is the purest, freest gift there is. However embracing the fullness of His majesty we are to change our ways. Our ways of thinking, imagining, doing, and expecting. And in changing these ways, there is a spiritual exchange as we die to our sinful ways and birth God's fruitful ways. The act of tithing produces juicy fruit. In God checking, testing, and assessing our hearts we may need to lose a thing or two, or many things in order to get right. In getting right, the journey towards purity will be beyond great measure.

Sow

God is the king of missions. His mission has always been consistent of peace, love, joy, purity. God knows nothing opposed to His mission. God knows nothing opposed to His perfect will. We are either for Him, one hundred percent, or against Him. There is no in between business with our heavenly Father. Respect is a must. And yes, God is about His business, His Kingdom realm. God created us for His purpose and thus knows our every need and desire. We need not to doubt His way. He too knows our struggles and weaknesses as He sees over the earth. God is God, His ability to hear each prayer and see each soul is grand. His incredible nature could never be fathomed by our brains. Our time of worship, praise, and prayer are forms of sowing as we build up our spirit. When we hear clearly, we understand what seeds to sow, blessengs to contend and curses to break.

In speaking of missions, God uses us to fulfill His call. We are to sow to reap all His blessings. God graciously gifts us with His spiritual powers; we need only to exercise our authority within Him. God is regularly blessing us with ideas to grow and develop our spiritual gifts. God is also regularly blessing us with strategy to become purer, as we are divinely placed in the right place at the right time. As God observes our heart of perseverance and determination through faithful sowing (and praying), he fulfills our request according to His will.

God's mission involves our pure obedience. As God gives us an assignment to fulfill, we immediately sow where He calls us to do so. In respecting the levels to God's stewardship, we respectfully recognize that sowing is a level. Developing faith that produces works is music to God's ears. God desires our trust wholeheartedly, that we not rely on nothing but His every word. He desires us to complete the unthinkable, the impossible.

> Our Father in heaven, Hallowed be Your name. Your kingdom come. Your will be done. On earth as it is in heaven. Give us this day our daily bread. And forgive us our debts, As we forgive our debtors. And do not lead us into temptation, But deliver us from the evil one. For Yours is the kingdom and the power and the glory forever. Amen. (Matt. 6:10-13 NKJV)

Prophetess Leslie once expressed how the Bible is conditional, this timely expression supports the fact that there are levels to growth, and becoming pure. We can only be emotionally healthy as we become spiritually healthy. Write this down and prayerfully the highlighter has been used wisely. We cannot be emotionally healthy if we are not spiritually healthy. We cannot focus on one aspect of God without the others. We cannot create our own terms of God; His terms have been predestined for us.

Radiate

God's love radiates over all. God is our ray of sunshine. God is also our refuge. As the theme continues, we can only be because of Him. Our faith becomes stronger as we reside in the presence of God. Wherever God calls us, there we shall be. As God spirit leads, we are taken deeper than we can ever wonder, imagine, fathom. To radiate is to trust.

The trust factor with our heavenly father will allow us to radiate. Trust is built as we allow it to be built. Our integral God demands our trust as well, what blasphemy to seek Him only because of a moment and then return to sin. Trust is naturally developed as we open our Bible, our personal guide to God's wisdom. Our personal guide to God's Kingdom lies in between the many stories within His word. We radiate as we learn from those who were against God. We radiate as we gain inspiraftion from those who were for God. Those who were for God and experienced mind blowing miracles and wonders all by God's grace. As we seek God within we choose to trust His way over our way. Trailblazing requires trust in our God almighty as well as our trust to obey His way.

To obey is to rise. Rise, we are to arise. We are to arise with God and radiate like never before. We are to bloom where we are planted. Bloom and embrace the uniqueness of who we are. God provides us with every tool and resource of strength within us. God uses us for His mysterious ways, He chooses us specifically to be captivated by others. God is creator, and His creative ways allow us to radiate in various ways and forms. He has specially handpicked us to bare His fruit. As we hear and obey, we are able to radiate across nations carrying His fruit as He waters every single seed we plant. God makes all the impossible possible.

Radiance is soulful. Radiance is joyful. Radiance is pure and precious. There is only one of us. May we treat ourselves like the jewel, gem, diamond, pearl and pot of gold we are. When we wake, think to radiate. When we step out, think to radiate. When we speak, think to radiate. When we think, think to radiate. To radiate is a profoundness of vibration that is felt by presence and observed through interaction. To radiate is a gentle yet strong excitement that breads life. God radiates through us, and His radiance births our testimonies as we journey to purity. Who we were before God and the radiant soul we have become with God is a story worth sharing. We learn to blossom and blossom some more. We learn to not only strive for greatness but thrive beyond greatness. We learn to be a light, be free , to overcome and become.

Be doers of the word and not hearers only, deceiving yourselves. (Jm. 1:22 NKJV)

Becoming Godly is radiant. God ignites the soulful flame from deep within our spirit. Becoming pure is radiant. God's voice is clearer, and our choices are wiser. We decide to be purer, we commit to being pure, and we fuel our mind with God's word to embrace a Godly lifestyle full of radiance. We radiate as we become doers of God's Holy guide; as we hear His voice we obey His righteousness.

Radiance is becoming like God, being in a secret place with Him. Him and us against the world. Radiance is being made new, being made like God. The conditions in becoming like God is fulfilling purpose in all aspects of our life, as a child, as a teacher, as a steward, as a coach, as an athlete, as an artist, as a parent, and the list goes on. "We must have a Godly vision in order to fulfill our purpose." (Osei, 2020).

We can only radiate having being in closeness with our God, learning our assignment on earth. Our heavenly Father is our greatest father teaching us how to become more like him, getting our mind, body, soul, heart, and spirit right to radiate His nation.

God's Spirit allows us to have a vision. We must understand the reason God placed us on earth in order to have drive and focus for each day, making every day purposeful. We have been divinely created and called for a specific purpose, heaven awaits us. And with God our vision is restored. While without God our vision is distorted. May we seek God's vision and see in the spirit. (Habakkuk 2: 2-5) May we live in His Heavenly realm, and not among lukewarm *business*. May we allow the Holy Spirit to radiate within us, thy kingdom come. May we allow Christ to manifest through us. May we share everything with and trust Him with our lives, in which He has given us. May we trust in His grace, and His grace to radiate our lives.

> And Jesus increased in wisdom and stature, and in favor with God and men. (Lk. 2:52 NKJV)

Jesus has given us the standard of growth, wisdom, stature, and favor both in God and among men. We radiate as we understand and own our value in Christ. "When we encounter God it changes you. Encountering God is exchanging our body for His body." (Osei, 2020). We are cleansed from all unrighteousness as we allow God to purify our lives. We have to be in alignment with God to truly understand our value. Jewel, Precious Jewel God's promises are greater than any mental (emotional) attacks or struggles. We grow through radiance with God's grace and power.

We must believe; we are what we think. We think as though we are. Insecurity is a root after our own heart. Fearfulness holds us back from radiating and will continue to stomp our growth; This is the enemy's way of attacking our imagination. Therefore, we have to always be prepared and regularly purified. For some perspective, God forms fire, lightning, earthquakes, thunder, and pestilence. (Lk 21:11 NKJV).

Montgomery also explains that social media is a blessing but if we are broken then it's a curse. This line is something serious. Imagine how lives could radiate through social media, purely and genuinely so. Imagine the opposite, how our lives could transpire gloominess and darkness. This latter is not God. There are too beautiful, women and men of God connected to all forms of social media. The blessings are endless as we have amazing resources to level up right at our finger times.

May our social media be purely connected with God's ministers, prophets (ess), and leaders. May we binge God's spiritual food virtually and mores personally. May our Lord reign, remain near, and reign forever in our lives. May our heart be clean to allow radiance manifest abundantly. May our heart, intentions, visions, be right before God. May we be still, and learn real stillness. "God moves on His time as a reflection of our heart" (Osei, 2020). May we always be still and ready to be radiated by God's goodness. May we give up our life and choose to take up Christ's cross daily (Matt. 16:24-25). May we step our game up, and radiate. May God's love free and radiate us.

By God's might and spirit we are supernatural, we are radiant, trailblazers. Alignment with God's bible-sense is greater than any *common* sense. His wisdom is perfection. May we be elevated, magnified, through God's word and revelation. The enemy tries to take our appetite, our peace. However, our mind, body, soul, are designed by God for His perfect, divine alignment. In purifying our life, cleansing is encouraged one step at a time, one day at a time. Only with cleansing and meditating on His holy word can we truly radiate.

Godly meditation is reading, processing, and gaining revelation of God's wisdom. God communicates through His holy scripts to console our life. When God provides revelation, what a sweet, sweet day it is in the city. And the revelation of His spiritual gift, tongues, is literally pure chills. *Ooh wee*! Praying God's scripture is essential in allowing them to become our reality. Praying God's heavenly language is special in allowing His Holy Spirit to intercede our prayer. (Romans8:26 KJV)

Being baptized with the precious gift of the Holy Spirit is a wonderful experience, radiating spiritually for real. (Acts 2:1-5 KJV)Speaking in God's perfect language is an utterance of oneness with His Spirit. Spiritual revelation of the Holy tongue brings us pure oneness, with an overwhelming joy. Our spiritual tongue allows us to also succeed in times of "warfare" dodging any bullets, equipping us with His full armor. Our spiritual tongue is God's heavenly expression and language, only He understands completely. God has pre ordered and pre assigned His angels to rightfully act on our behalf.

We must be willing for the Holy Spirit to intercede in our lives. As the Holy Spirit lives within us, we have the luxury to become whole with our heavenly creator and live in a righteous consciousness with Jesus Christ. Literally God and the Holy Spirit has gifted us with the perfect prayer opportunity while edifying our soul. (1Cor 14:1-5).

> The One whom God has sent to represent him will speak the words of God, for God has poured out upon him the fullness of the Holy Spirit without limitation. (Jhn. 3:34 TPT)

Hearing God is the absolute fulfilling sentiment that ever lived. God speaks often, for instance when we are having impure sex and He is nodding our thoughts opposing the affair. Or when we are considering and tempting to commit harmful activity to self or others. He speaks to warn and protect us in these particular situations to prevent scenarios of single parenting, abuse, abortion, heartbreak, or incarceration.

Heartbreak is mentioned various times as *feelings* have a huge impact on our decisions. At times these decisions change our life. Other times, our heart is so hard because of rejection that we feel burdened. We are burdened from a cycle of loss whether death or circumstance. And as a result we have lost faith and hope in people, sometimes even in God. "Possession is greater than oppression; we must pray and allow God to deliver us from oppression" (Osei, 2020). We either allow the world to enter our heart and become impure, or we allow God to enter our heart and become pure.

Reflection

- What (areas aspects) will you focus on trailblazing through this month?
- Pray for God to reveal who or what ministry He desires you to join and sow into?
- Read John 3
- Read 1 Corinthians 1
- Document your wins of overcoming temptations.
- Document your wins of hearing God's voice, write what He says.
- Document ways you radiated towards becoming purer.

13

"THE CALL"

My sheep hear My voice, and I know them, and they follow Me. And I give them eternal life, and they shall never perish; neither shall anyone snatch them out of My hand. **John 10:27-8 NKJV**

Hear Him, know Him, and follow Him. This is a sweet short yet mighty prayer within itself. Pray, lovingly, precious Father, may I hear you, know you, follow you. Pray with loving eagerness to desire more, to be more, and to pursue more with God. Our purity is our right. Our purity is our call. God is the answer to our call. We embrace life to its fullest purpose as we are pure before God. As we answer God's call to purify us, we become one. God is one call away, one call away of guiding us to overcome sexual imaginations, sexual immoralities, and sexual pains. We have freedom of unlimited, speed dial calling.

In our own pure accent, with our own pure personality, God is overjoyed to hear from us. As we think of sex, call. As we desire sex, call. As we have a flashback of a sexual encounter, call. Whether our call begins, "Yo, God, cleanse my mind ASAP" or "Oh loving and precious God, I beg you to take these lustful thoughts out of my head now" or "Aye yo pops these sexual thoughts have to go" or even "Father God, what's really God, I pray for immediate miraculously healing over my sexual scars please. May I experience your spiritual cleansing." or "God, this is an emergency, I repent, change me, renew me" or "Oh God, may your angels cover me as I sleep" or "Father God, with your power break every stronghold of each sexual relationship from my past" All in Jesus might name. In growing through and overcoming our sinful nature, we must faithfully believe each prayer we share with God. As we pray, we must also faithfully say them repeatedly until we achieve them. And praying the word of God is our defense against static, poor reception, bad service, which also raises the volume in our call.

God is our mindfulness as we are still. The saying *it's a two way street* surely applies. God gives freely as His nature, however to embrace the fullness of His glory we are responsible for answering the call to salvation, call to purity, call to freedom. We are responsible for receiving the call, and acknowledging our impurities. While we are still, in His presence knowing that He is God, our almighty God we hear clearly. God completes His call with love. Are we willing to take the call, is the number one question, to be free of mental, physical, sexual, emotional, spiritual bondage? Are we willing to trail blaze, focus, purify our entire life to gain total freedom? Are we willing to guard our hearts, protect our peace to embrace pure joy? Are we willing to abstain from impure doings, relations, encounters to honor God, our creator, Father, transformer, restorer?

Be in the world but not of the world. (Romans 12;2 NKJV) Be okay to be different from the world, be okay to stand out from the world. God created us different, He is our creator. God created us to be different and embrace our differences, one of the quadrillions of beauties of His divinity. We are equally beautifully different, yet equally loved by Abba Father. And He said, "Abba, Father, all things are possible for You. Take this cup away from me; nevertheless, not what I will, but what You will" (Mk. 14:36 NKJV) Even in the moments of trial, despair, sorrow, God's gracious will, will be done. As we are pure before God, He works all things out for our greater good; God is God, Abba Father. He takes care of the lost desiring to be found, the impure desiring to be pure.

We are meant to create a beautiful, pure life given our uniqueness. Our gifts, talents, passions, stories are uniquely designed to bring glory to God's name. As we execute our divine purpose, we add value to His Kingdom. We are meant to stand out and shine bright for His glory. We are meant to answer the call of purity. In answering God's call we surrender our thoughts, businesses, relations, dreams to His Lordship. God's Kingdom is pure, in answering His call; we are choosing to be pure.

God needs total Lordship of every part of our life, our spiritual, emotional, physical, and financial health must be surrendered in the hands of Abba Father. In order for God to fulfill greatness within us we need to allow Him to purify and transform us. The condition of our heart needs next level deep cleaning, not just on a Sunday as we spend to spring clean or not just a "word" from a sermon here and there. God needs us, all of us. Purity requires more than a spring cleaning day and listening to someone preach. Similar to the factors of unstable relationships whether due to miscommunication, abuse or adultery we hinder our relationship with God when we lack communication and faithfulness. Miscommunication with God is a lack of surrender (particularly emotionally when addressing purity) and abusing God is a lack of reverence for his grace. While cheating on God is a lack of quality time spent reading His word and hearing His voice.

Making God the Lord of our lives is choosing to be transformed from the inside out. Our imagination has been playing us for far too long. The time has approached for us to become relentless in what we allow to enter our mind. The time has approached for us to become fearless in how we commit to Abba Father. Reading God's word is one commitment; as we meditate (study and observe) His scripture with pure understanding we naturally adapt to a fearlessness of believing and achieving greatness (JOSHUA 1:8 KJV). God's word must take root within; the word of God has the ability to remove old weeds as pure roots develop. Making God Lord over every aspect of our life is allowing Him to uproot unrighteousness and root righteousness. At times we may not be aware of our infertile ground (life) but God graciously reveals our impurities real quick as we call unto Him.

Becoming emotionally healthy is a reflection of spiritual health. In becoming spiritually healthy we must learn to discern God's voice and all Him to speak in our spirit. As the Lord our God speaks in our spirit, we must obey. Learning to hear Abba clearly directly correlates with reading His word with Godly revelation. As we pray His word, God graces us with purity and peace. The glory in His power is the most *beautifulest*, coolest, craziest thing. Our lens truly becomes purer.

To call unto God is inviting His presence, allowing Him to tend directly to our critical conditions. His critical points are designed to save and heal our hearts in this vulnerable moment. We are responsible to trust and believe. We are responsible to focus on one day at a time, not worrying about the next day (Matt. 6:34 KJV). May the revelation of scripture be upon us, that clarity and truth dwell among us?

Pure surrender is developed from reading God's word and living God's word. Only then do we recognize the difference between *right* and righteous. We love to be loved. We love to be protected. We love to feel loved. We love to feel protected. Because we are children of God, we naturally are subject to love. Calling unto God's love allows us to experience more of Him, as He has His way in our life.

Revelation of God's word, revelation of righteousness, encourages us to speed dial heaven's digits. God gladly responds with pure joy. Because of His emperor, authority and character we need not to play, standards are set (again as a healthy, strong relationship should) to guard against being taken advantage of. Our call to Abba is a representation of closing the door of sin and entering the door of peace, love, grace, mercy. Entering God's gates is an experience of His powerful presence.

Only then do we acknowledge God's voice, and truly discern His wisdom as well as strategy. Holy discernment, wisdom, and strategy is all you need in this life of sin. Not *you and your "girlfriend"* as Jay-Z sang, that is very incorrect. We must be down to ride with our Heavenly Father, God, and Abba to the absolute very end. He is the call we have all been waiting and longing for. God has desired us as we have been seeking Him, and we did not even know it. Never-minding the status of your relationship in life or with God, there is always greater.

With this being said, God in actuality speaks to us because He loves and adores us; when He speaks to warn and protect us is because He knows better than we do. God created communication and quality time. Hence we long for just quality relationships; God has predestined the standards for a Godly marriage and pure relationships. And only He can prepare us for one on earth. Trial and error in the sex game is not the preparation, *okay*. The call is ours, as He is our provider and the only pure source that fulfills our every need and desire.

God loves us more than we will ever know. The call is ours to make whether we choose to trust His perfect way and will for our lives or rather to trust our imperfect way. God is in control, through His words He created a perfect world. Living to struggle and fight to gain control over our lives because of heartbreak and trust issues will cause burnout.

Once Upon A Time

Godddd, I am in awe! I am in awe! I cannot contain my joy. The purest, sweetest, beautifulest, specialist moment I have ever experienced. Thank you for guiding and directing my paths. Thank you for your nearness. Thank you for allowing me to experience this special moment with you. The joy of being still on your chest, in your embrace is the sweetest feeling. I am forever overjoyed by your goodness, your perfection. You squeezed my hands, I am speechless at this. Thank you for hearing my heart's cry and bringing me where you are. Thank you for orchestrating divine relationships. Thank you for every single lesson that I have faced where you continuously teach me perseverance. Thank you for your glory oh Father. Thank you for your favor. I am forever grateful to be held by you, my king. I am forever grateful for your Holy Spirit, your spiritual strength.

Thank you for your omnipresence. I want to forever be where you are oh God. Thank you for holding my hands. Thank you for holding me. Thank you for filling me up with pure peace and love, thank you for your overflow of goodness. Thank you for embracing my soul. Thank you for saving me. I want to be where you are, oh Lord, I have to be where you are, dwelling in your perfect presence. Thank you for skin to skin contact oh God. I am infatuated by your goodness, your perfection. I will forever soak in your love. Thank you for devine intervention, causing me to learn from your Kingdom builders. Thank you Lord God for Apostle Dominic Osei and Prophetess Lesley Osei. Thank you Lord God for Prophetess Tiphani Montgomery. Bless them richly oh Lord. Thank you for peace oh God. Thank you for your perfect peace Father God. I only want and desire and need to be where you are. Thank you for revelation and wisdom. Skin to skin contact has changed my entire life. I am on a-whole-nother level father and I am just in awe. I lift my praise to you oh

God. Thank you for rest. Thank you for joy. Thank you for filling my cup oh God, thank you for making me whole.

God gently squeezed and held my hands. The most pure experience we can ever experience. I was introduced to the beauty of skin to skin contact and later learned another referenced term as soaking. During the first few days of April 2020, I had my absolute first skin to skin contact experience with my Father God. The moment was surreal, magnificently beautiful. I lay to the altar near my bedside with soft music in the background. I had just finished writing for the day and Holy Spirit pulled me to the floor. After the revelation the night before via Instagram live and all the sweetness shared, my body could not resist. My soul could not wait.

The moment of complete stillness was yet so powerful. As I lay on my belly, forehead low on the small pillow, I melted into God's heavenly realm. I literally was floating on the clouds of His enormous belly. This was my moment, the moment I desired forever, to be embraced by my heavenly father. The purest love we could ever imagine. Unaware of the time nor the day, my palms faced upward. My body was soft, my face was soft with the most refreshing smile within. I then felt a gentle tug to my hand, a grip that hugged each hand softly. Then I whispered "God" and my only response was tears of joy and gratitude. The saddest I felt was the time I had missed being near to my Father. This moment was so special and is forever dear to my heart.

* * *

To me, the call is holding hands with God. The call represents God's nearness and desire for oneness. I could never fathom life alone because my life is in His hands. God holds my hands, even as I write or type. God is here holding, guiding, and comforting me gracefully. We are broken gracefully, and made whole purely because of God's everlasting love. There will never be a day that passes without intimacy with my loving Father. My first exposure to skin *to skin contact is the sweetest memory I'll forever cherish. I lay on God's chest free of worry, schedule, lack, uncertainty. I lay on His chest excited and humbled to be there forever. Literally, I had no desire to leave His side.*

Our lack of discernment and knowledge of God causes us to move in defense. Often we also are irresponsible in our decisions. God is also a gardener among His many Lordships. Think of when people question how we became good at certain things, and we respond that "I just am, I have always been good at it." Great, this perfect example of God is just God. He is superior, the superior, emperor who created heaven and earth. He has always been and will forever be. Back to healing, without acknowledging the roots of rejection, our control mechanism strives to redeem hope by indulging in harmful self situations. Talk about *rootssss*.

God compares us to a tree, specifically a fruit tree (Jhn. 15 NKJV). And as shared in Chapter 6, Focus, God specifically aligns us to a fruit tree in reference to maturity. Our gardener is in the business of producing the perfect, purest, juiciest garden. Our tree becomes ripened through His pruning and weeding. God begins to prune through the branches of our tree as we make the call knowing that with God we become. Realizing that the call to God enriches us emotionally (mentally), physically, financially, spiritually we immediately dial His line of salvation.

As we make the call of emergency for weeding to produce the current season of fruit, God answers speedily. Though time is of the essence in this process; the timelines of weeding and uprooting is not an application of a cotton ball, band aid, first aid kit as conducted by the emergency medical technicians we are familiar with. God treats each of our lives (or our emergencies) in relation to a tree with damaged roots. Considering an actual tree, its roots run very deep given the maturity. A tree could not be if the roots were not strong and healthy. Righteous roots are also sown within as we read God's word and experience His wonders.

The entire dialogue of roots is another whole book. The roots and conversations are equally deep. *Deep, deep.* God is so amazing in this way in creating relationships between us and lessons of His nature. Following a study conducted by Day S. & Wiseman E. (2009), they shared that "a six-inch tree could have roots out from the trunk as far as nineteen feet. Studies for mature trees are fewer, but suggest that this ratio is smaller for older trees." No matter our physical stature, God is ready to equip our spiritual stature with an abundance of righteousness. As Godly roots are sowed, branches and fruits of life are produced. Another fun fact: the greatest reported depth to which a tree's roots have penetrated is four-hundred feet by a Wild Fig tree at Echo Caves, near Ohrigstad, Mpumalanga, South Africa (Neighbors, 2020).

Wow, right! How impressively, incredible is this detail. So why the fun fact? Thanks for asking. God refers to us as trees of life, and by His gracious gardening miracles we produce supernatural greatness. This also requires His steady pruning. A tree of four-hundred feet roots does not occur overnight; in actuality, trees grow to this caliber after many, many years, many more than our lifespan. We knew that, right.

However, a Godly perspective is critical. And this fun fact gets better, in Nahum 3:12 NKJV. God said "all your strongholds are fig trees with ripened figs, and if they are shaken they fall into the mouth of the eater." Now if this is not, wow. With this being said, a stronghold can either be good or evil. God clearly states that He too will shake us of an evil stronghold, a sin aiming to keep us in bondage. God's judgment rules and shakes the fruit of our tree to the ground as easy as ripen fruit fall (Guzik, 2020). In scripture, God makes reference to strongholds as sin rooted in satan's demise ie. fear and pride though they are nothing to Him .(2 cor.

10:4) Although seemingly a stronghold for us to deal with it is a slight situation for Him to handle.

Furthermore, fig trees are also mentioned forty-three times in the noted version (last fun fact pertaining to trees and figs), while referenced to strength, power, intelligence, life. Fig trees are something special, significant. This is pure Godincidence. God is our strong tower for purity (2 Samuel 22:3 ;Psalm 18:2) . Allowing God to be our strongtower over allowing sin to be our stronghold is our determinant factor of purity. God is the strongtower we need to develop ripened figs, deeply rooted fig trees. God gives us strength, power, intelligence, life. God strengthens us with the means to overcome sinful temptation, endure through challenge, and experience His power.

Jewel, precious Jewel, it is of the same importance for our roots to be pruned as it is for our soil to be moistened. Our roots will also be unstable and unhealthy if our soil is dry. As seeds are planted in our life through reading the Holy word and God using others to develop our knowledge, He graciously waters. Another gardening (tree) source notes the care needed in identifying a soil line of a plant. This identification is crucial "to allow for the plant to be measured at the same depth as it was grown or slightly deeper" (Unknown, 2020). Therefore, with care, we need to identify where our soil line lies. We also need to identify if we are in it to win it. Our choice to call unto God is choosing to steadily grow, and choosing to not call unto God is choosing to steadily plateau.

Seeds are either planted in dry or moist soil. Depending how dry or moist our soil is reflects the amount of water we are in need of. God is our gardener, hydrator, and pruner. Additionally, Unknown, (2020) stated that the pruning of damaged roots occurs above the break, as well as crossing roots or unusually long roots. Below the break of the root there is still hope as we make the call. There is also hope in discovering a jewel as well beneath the surface.

In John 15 NKJV, Jesus also assures that the world would hate us because of our love for God. We win some, we lose some. Though pleasing God is true victory, whereas pleasing men is only a loss if we choose to care about their *feelings* over God's commands. This said, as trouble comes our way, which it will, we pray moreso proactively . We know to call because that is God's love language. "When trouble comes, the Lord is our stronghold. We have a place to run, be strengthened and protected. The Lord is a stronghold to those that are in trouble" (Guzik, 2020). Sadly, shall we not make the call, and surrender in claiming our place of a child before our heavenly Father, when trouble comes, we have no place to go. But the child of God always has a refuge." "The name of the Lord is a strong tower, the righteous runneth into it, and is safe" (Guzik, 2020). Then he declares, and he knoweth them that trust in him The Lord *is* good, a stronghold in the day of trouble; and he knoweth them that trust in him (Nah. 1:7 NKJV).

Control is a tough (hard) cookie that is if we aim to be the controller. However, control is a soft cookie as we allow God to be the controller, His nature. Having to take on the 'world' solo is tiring and boring. Believe the writer, for real. There is a survival, instant mode that takes place. There is also a trust factor where everyone is untrustworthy, the idea of *guilty until proven innocent* in this case. However, as we grow with God, He increases our portion. As we call unto God, He brings us joy.

May we be strengthened by His grace and mercy. May we have a pure heart, mind, body, soul, spirit. May we fervently seek God, His love, peace, forgiveness. God knows our hearts and assures us that there is a narrow gate to righteousness, while a wide gate to unrighteousness (Matthew 7:13-14 KJV). Similar to the adopted, expressed saying of man, whereas the road less travelled is not the joyful one. Though societal opinions tend to glorify unrighteousness, spiritual truths celebrate righteousness and eternity.

Jesus Christ desires to know us, to have a relationship with us, an individual bond. God has preordained the plans for our life. Fulfilling life with our Heavenly Father is a pure satisfaction in knowing we are living with His power and authority. Living according to God's ordinance is soothing and rewarding. Hearing God's voice is the only call we need to prosper.

God's voice is power. God's voice is the only confidence and confirmation we need. God's voice is the GPS to navigate us towards the relationship meant for us, the friendships meant for us, the business endeavor meant for us, the people meant to minister to us. Our GPS is always accurate and therefore never fails. Our GPS is the key to every Godly marriage, friendship, financial investment, and prosperous move.

I can do all things through Christ who strengthens me. (Phil. 4:13 ESV)

May God create in us a pure, clean, and solid heart. May He enhance our faith and strengthen our hope. May we always seek God and plead that He sets us free. May doubt be removed, may confusion be removed, and may fear be removed from our mind, heart, body, soul, spirit. May our faith in Christ allow us to do all things through His spiritual might.

May our names be written in the lamb's book of Christ, may we embrace the body of Christ. May we meet in heaven knowing that we faithfully love our Lord God with our entire heart, constantly let our heart to be pruned, and loyally live to please God. May God acknowledge our call and journey to purity. May God acknowledge us, well done, we indeed live as good and faithful servants producing plentiful fruit with the gracious gifts and talents He has blessed us with.

Finally, you are a Precious Jewel. You are a pure, precious Jewel. Your Jewel may have been damaged but you are a precious Jewel. Your Jewel may have been lost but you are a precious Jewel. Your Jewel may be robbed, used, abused but you are still a precious Jewel says the Lord. You may have been cut, cut deep, shattered but you are still a precious Jewel. Your Jewel may have been embodiment in a sinful stronghold but God's stronghold is mightier, purer. You may have been lost, lonely, longing, but you are still a precious Jewel.

God is perfect. God is pure. God is purpose. God is precious. God made us in His perfect image, with pure purposeful intentions. We are a part of His masterpiece. We are a masterpiece. In knowing God, God is love. He created us in love, for love. And growing in love with God is the perfect love story.

Spiritual gifts are everything in this love story. While studying in Kingdom Entrepreneur University, Montgomery (2020) shared a great diagram listing each gift and its respective category. There are 3 main categories including vocal, revelatory, and power. Vocal gifts consist of speaking tongues, interpreting tongues, and prophesying. Revelatory gifts consist of knowledge, wisdom, spiritual discernment, and power gifts consist of faith, healing, and miracles. When we don't know, we just don't know.

However, God gifted us with these incredible wonders to experience His wonders. Each gift edifies us and draws us nearer to God. Speaking in tongues fills our physical room with God's spiritual presence as the Holy Spirit utters through us. Interpreting tongues allows for deeper revelation of each utterance. Prophesying is God allowing Jesus Christ us to foresee past the present, preparing self and others for personal or communal situations. Knowledge and wisdom is of a great sacrificial heart, focusing on studying fervently God's scripture, gaining the purest understanding. Discerning Godly spirits and evil ones equips us for success while guards us from destruction. Seeing and smelling when people, places, things are pure at heart or not is important. While faith, healing, and miracles change lives as God's spiritual grace works through our physical actions.

God is still in the business of miracles as He was and as He always will be. Faith knows the word in order to be encouraged and be filled with a pure mind. We are more than enough, with God's divine strategy. We are spiritually wise and naturally intelligent with every thought to the obedience of Christ. We must have the artillery of guard, ready for a sweet war. We are God's soldiers on His battlefield.

Calling unto God will power us to build our life towards the vision He gives us. As we pray about the vision God shows, we are to seek strategy to allow God to work through us, for us, and make it happen. Reading and praying is our strategy to conquer this life. Allowing the peace of God to settle our mind, while having faith, hope, trust in God will settle our souls. Keeping ourselves in the presence of God consists of constant worship and praise, as well as scripture retention. Engulfing ourselves in the presence of God will greatly enable our journey of purity. The enemy is insulted by God; therefore we use our weapons of prayer and praise to confuse him, override sin.

> For the weapons of our warfare are not carnal but mighty in God for pulling down strongholds, casting down arguments and every high thing that exalts itself against the knowledge of God, bringing every thought into captivity to the obedience of Christ. (2 Cor. 10:4-5 NKJV)

We have the same Spirit of faith that is described in the scriptures when it says, "First I believed, then I spoke in faith" (2 Cor. 4:13 NKJV). So we also first believe then speak in faith. We do this because we are confident that He who raised Jesus Christ will raise us up with Him, and together we will all be brought into His Holy presence. Yes, all things work for our enrichment so that more of God's marvelous grace will spread to more and more people. God specially instilled gifts within us to sow into others in building His Kingdom.

For even though our outer being gradually wears out, our inner being is renewed every single day. We view our slight, short-lived troubles in the light of eternity. We see our difficulties as the substance that produces for us an eternal glory far beyond all comparison. Our main focus and attention is not on what is seen but on what is unseen, (Heb. 11:1 NKJV). For what is seen is temporary, but the unseen realm is eternal (2 Cor. 4:13-18 NKJV) .

Praying scriptures as such are even more profound as we personalize them. Call unto God personally, desiring a pure heart in order to make pure choices. Jesus says, I am a true sprouting vine, and the farmer who tends the vine is my Father. He cares for the branches connected to me by lifting and propping up the fruitless branches and pruning every fruitful branch to yield a greater harvest. The words I have spoken over you have already cleansed you. So you must remain in life-union with me, for I remain in life-union with you. For as a branch severed from the vine will not bear fruit, so your life will be fruitless unless you live your life intimately joined to mine. "I am the sprouting vine and you're my branches. As you live in union with me as your source, fruitfulness will stream from within you—but when you live separated from me you are powerless." (Jhn. 15:1 NKJV).

This love call will have us pure in no time, just wait and see. Our prayer request can begin, loving, precious God I desire to be a true sprouting vine, oh Lord may you tend to my vines, they need to be purified. Thank you for caring for me and propping up fruitless branches, pruning every fruitful branch. Thank you for cleansing me. Father God may you teach me your way, how to remain in life union with you. We continue to share our heart with God as we meditate on His goodness, and boom infiltration begins. Desire more, pray more, and eat more (of His daily bread of course).

> "But if you live in life-union with me and if my words live powerfully within you—then you can ask whatever you desire and it will be done. When your lives bear abundant fruit, you demonstrate that you are my mature disciples who glorify my Father!" (Jhn. 15:7-8 TPT)

> You didn't choose me, but I've chosen and commissioned you to go into the world to bear fruit. And your fruit will last, because whatever you ask of my Father, for my sake, he will give it to you!" (Jhn. 15:16 TPT)

God is the source of our strength, providing peace in any storm. GPS is purely available as we allow prayer and discernment to facilitate our every decision. As we develop a Godly spirit, pure, mind, body, soul, GPS will be more valuable. We must desire all of his presence, more of His Spirit, more of His love, more of His mercy.

> "In other words, it was through the Anointed One that God was shepherding the world, not even keeping records of their transgressions, and he has entrusted to us the ministry of opening the

door of reconciliation to God. We are ambassadors of the Anointed One who carry the message of Christ to the world, as though God were tenderly pleading with them directly through our lips. So we tenderly plead with you on Christ's behalf, "Turn back to God and be reconciled to him." For God made the only one who did not know sin to become sin for us, so that we who did not know righteousness might become the righteousness of God through our union with Him" (2 Cor. 5:19-21 TPT)

God's steadfast love endures forever. As we appreciate, understand, and experience that God's love is perfect, life becomes the *beautifullest*, purest journey.

He who finds a wife finds a good thing, And obtains favor from the Lord. (Prv. 18:22 NKJV)

He who finds a good wife finds a good thing says the Lord, as He delights for us to secure our destiny within. Finding a wife is the role of a mature, Godly man. A male's role includes pursuing the woman God has hand picked for him. While a woman's role includes waiting expectantly for the man God has desired for her to have. God knows the desire of our heart, and rightfully fulfills our desires. As our desires stem from pure motives we can be assured they are of God. God's hand picked couples are equally yoked and faithfully committed to His will (2 Cor. 2:14 NKJV). God's hand picked couples are destined to be at the right place at the right time to meet and receive God's confirmation of blessing.

God gives us the way and shows us the way to live. God provides us with the right tools, resources, and contacts to achieve righteousness. As we pray, believe, and read God's word, we excitedly develop a Godly mentality. Adapting a Godly mindset allows us to have a Godly perspective, and as a result allows us to make pure decisions. Humility allows us to hear and gain God's wisdom. God gives us the way through His wisdom, which protects us from sleeping with and marrying fools (Prv. 12:20 NKJV). God shows us the way through His holy spirit, which guides us towards righteousness. God warns us that we perish with the lack of knowledge. We perish as we have sex casually, ignore God's way deliberately, and disregard God's call for salvation. God is a visionary, as we have sex with no vision; we set ourselves up to perish (Prv. 29:18 NKJV).

> My people are destroyed for lack of knowledge. Because you have rejected knowledge, I also will reject you from being priest for Me; Because you have forgotten the law of your God, I also will forget your children. (Hos. 4:6 NKJV)

God also desires to hear from couples, individually and mutually. May we continue to embrace God's blessings as they come and remain in perfect harmony with His perfection. May we continue to embrace God's power in purity and security. May we continue to call unto God even more as we recognize our purpose and power in our single and married season. May we continue to seek God's wisdom and discern His perfect will. As married couples, our children also are dependent on our obedience. Our children are dependent on our righteousness, to benefit from God's goodness. God desires to use us and our family for greatness as we desire to be pure and call unto Him. When we know God for who He really is, it affects our conduct. "Where there is no knowledge of God, no conviction of his omnipresence and omniscience, we prevail" (Guzik, 2020).

While the enemy has waved sex in our face, God has waved purity in our face. Sadly our flesh is weak and chooses the enemy's sinful ways over God's faithful ways. Physically having sex while not spiritually being whole is such a no, no. The negative impacts on our soul are deep, and as we shake our head, sadly saying real deep. God intended for sex to be sacred and built on a healthy, Godly foundation. God intended sex to be intimate, special, pure, between His two precious Jewels in order to become one. In order to have peaceful, pure relationships, we have to be led by God's direction. May we not allow ourselves to be less then and strive to become more than with God. May we not allow ourselves to miss the opportunity of wholeness in our precious lifetime. May we not allow ourselves to be insecure. And may we understand God's design and intent for becoming whole and pure before Him, that we may be restored and revived. May we understand that as we align with God's divine design, we become pure. May we embrace the fullness of our lifelong journey with God, conditioning a perfect heart to be pure before God?

> For you are the temple of the living God. As God has said: "I will dwell in them and walk among them. I will be their God, and they shall be My people." Therefore "Come out from among them and be separate, says the Lord. Do not touch what is unclean, and I will receive you. I will be a Father to you, and you shall be My sons and daughters, says the Lord Almighty. (2 Cor. 6:16-18 NKJV)

We are a temple, Jewel, precious Jewel. We were created to be holy, to live wholly. Our body is a sacred, sweet vessel. Our body is meant to be protected and cared for by God. Reestablishing our focus from all things sex related includes attention to achieving the fitness goals, building the business ideas, preparing the plentiful meals, and spending quality time with self which we have always desired. To treasure our temple requires respecting God's boundaries.

Sex naturally enables a soul tie of our mind, will, soul, hence God predestining marriages with our aligned, intended, purposeful soul tie (singular). Recognizing that we are a precious jewel, a holy temple, "we recognize and respect the boundary God as bestowed around sex for our protection" (Montgomery, 2020). God's boundaries are easy to respect as we part from distractions. God's temples are clean and pure with clear understanding that the wages of sin is death whether it is of a relationship, a gift, a child, or an opportunity.

Strong spiritual health allows us to manage and value our emotional health, physical health, nutritional health. We value our health because we are a gift and grace of God. Therefore, we exercise because God gifted us a beautiful body. We honor Him by maintaining strong, healthy muscles. We build the business we have pondered on. We prepare all the delightful plant based dishes that God provided us with. We spend more time developing quality time for self and Godly relationships.

Joy

> Be cheerful with joyous celebration in every season of life. Let joy overflow, for you are united with the Anointed One! (Phil. 4:4 TPT)

Some days are easy, some days are hard. Some days are encouraging, some days are discouraging. Choosing to thrive no matter the circumstances is choosing to persevere. And choosing to persevere is choosing joy. Ultimately choosing to thrive and persevere is choosing to be amazing.

God calls us to be amazing in all we do, be pure in all that we do. God calls us to glorify and honor him in all we do.

Despite being gracefully broken and experiencing weakness; when God says seek first His Kingdom (Matt. 6:33 NKJV), may we count it all joy (Jm. 1:2 NKJV). God's grace will always be upon us as we align with his perfect will. As He breaks us, His life and grace reign. Because we have been so damaged and destroyed we need to be broken down before we can be built up. We have to be broken down from sinful nature to gain a pure, spiritual nature. In order to develop emotional well being, God needs to rebuild us.

Joy is elevation in the power of God. Baptism is a part of elevation to bring us closer to God. Moves we make, things we do, and say requires sensitivity to God. The Holy Spirit is our sensitivity. When we understand the Spirit of God, we are sensitive to His timing. We live off of every word of God. Our flesh is weak but our spirit is willing, elevated in the power of God. We know how to respond and as we are in pure connectivity.

"There is cultivation in wilderness; we get nourishment, strength, power" (Jenkins, 2020). Isolation allows us to get ready and prepared for the assignment God has for us, marriages God has for us. Cultivation and growth is God's mission for us. May we not bypass the wilderness; God will always meet us there and show us how to proceed. Consistent prayer life allows us to make the right Godly decisions, build the right relationships, and move on the right timing of God. Prayer empowers us to experience pure joy in our everyday life.

This does not go without acknowledging and sympathizing with loss. In life we will experience hurdles. Some indeed are meant to strengthen us beyond our wildest dreams, beyond measure. While other lessons are just that, because God definitely knows that we are capable of overcoming.

The beauty is in the eye of the beholder, and also in the eye of the testimonial.(Isaiah 41:10 KJV) As we experience these hurdles and come out victorious, then others can truly be encouraged and blessed. Our stories are meant to give hope to the hopeless. Our stories are meant to shed light on others' darkness.

> God did not send his Son into the world to judge and condemn the world, but to be its Savior and rescue it! (Jhn. 3:17 TPT)

God reveals the characters, personalities, habits we have that are ungodly. When we draw near to God and build a healthier bond with God, we recognize that His way is greater than our way. God executed a great work in us if we allow Him to set us free. At times we may even become frustrated with the trials in the hours, the trials in the hours, the trials and the hours. However it's also too important to recognize our responsibility in the matter and how we could have responded or acted differently.

Reflection

God is:
Love
Sweet
Pure
Purpose
Precious

FINAL THOUGHTS

As a young child, our parent(s) strongly encouraged the importance of eating spinach (the worst tasting vegetable, so we thought, seemingly as a child), and any vegetable on our plate for that matter. We may have thought they were the most unloving person at the time yet the nature of our relationship was deeper than the purpose at the time. The nature of our relation could not allow us to withhold their love.

In this scenario, our minds were too immature to process that a vegetable of such taste was actually highly nutritious. (Advice : never give a child frozen, pre-packaged spinach). We were likely exposed to junk and sugary foods which damaged our taste buds to care for greens and beans. In reality our minds have been scarred with sin. The reality of giving up the life we are currently living, and trusting that there is better, strangely is hard to digest. We have accepted our reality as an accustomed way of life. Perceiving that we can truly experience more life, more freedom seems obscured. Though with knowledge we receive and experience pure peace, now all we desire to eat are fruits and vegetables. God is the highest of the highest nutritious values we will ever consume. The end is always more pleasing to God than the beginning (Osei, 2020).

May we have a heart of repentance knowing that our life has not been pleasing to our Heavenly Father, the one who created us to live sure and free of sin. May we reflect on ways to draw closer to God. Focus on God, level up prayer life. May we reflect on ways to build faith, honor God, and protect our jewel. May we love God, our loving, Heavenly Father with every piece our heart, soul, strength, mind.

REFERENCES

http://www.sandybarnursery.com/care-of-bareroot-trees.htm

https://www.blueletterbible.org/Comm/guzik_david/StudyGuide2017-Hsa/Hsa-4.cfm?a=866006

https://www.blueletterbible.org/Comm/guzik_david/StudyGuide2017-Nah/Nah-3.cfm?a=903012

Day S. & Wiseman E. (2009) https://www.deeproot.com/blog/blog-entries/how-wide-do-tree-roots-spread

http://www.rneighbors.org/projects/rneighborwoods/more-about-trees-2/missellaneous/world-records-bizarre-facts/

Leah Hager Cohen, (2013) I Don't Know: In Praise of Admitting Ignorance

https://www.merriam-webster.com/dictionary/leviathan
https://www.merriam-webster.com/dictionary/eagle

Britannica Jan 31, 2020 · In Isaiah 27:1, Leviathan is a serpent and a symbol of Israel's enemies, who will be slain by God. In Job ... " A symbol of God's power of creation"

https://www.britannica.com/topic/Leviathan-Middle-Eastern-mythology

https://www.lexico.com/en/definition/gemstone
https://adventure.howstuffworks.com/outdoor-activities/climbing/5-most-precious-stones.htm

"5 Most Precious Stones". *HowStuffWorks.com.* 2009-11-09. Archived from the original on 2014-11-06.
By Ali Somarin _03.20.2014
https://www.thermofisher.com/blog/mining/where-did-those-gemstones-come-from/
By Stellene Volandes
Sep 20, 2017
https://www.townandcountrymag.com/style/jewelry-and-watches/a12108751/pedigree-of-jewels/

https://msnucleus.org/membership/html/k-6/rc/minerals/4/rcm4_6a.html

https://www.google.com/search?q=jewel+and+plumeria+abstract+painting&tbm=isch&ved=2ahUKEwj035KqibHoAhWMA98KHYOZDtMQ2-cCegQIABAA&oq=jewel+and+plumeria+abstract+painting&gs_l=img.3...41782.42682..42850...0.0..0.130.753.7j1......0....1..gws-wiz-img.......35i39.nE4MNbXXeBA&ei=W-t4XrTGHYyH_AaDs7qYDQ&bih=661&biw=1280&client=firefox-b-d

https://www.openbible.info/topics/gods_love_for_us

https://ca.thegospelcoalition.org/columns/ad-fontes/5-surprising-things-that-the-bible-says-about-sex/

Lyles , Kristy
Anthony, Shawn
Montgomery, Tiphani
Osei, Dominic
Osei, Lesley
Jenkins , Kadesha

NOTES

Chapter 2

1. "A precious stone…" Lexico.com pg. 18
2. Blueletterblible.com pg. 20

Chapter 3

1. Sexual Partner Statistic pg. 24

Chapter 4

1. "Montgomery shared a live video" pg. 29
2. "A little backstory on the creation of jewels…" pg. 29

Chapter 5

1. Purpose is defined… pg. 35
2. Commune is defined… pg 35
3. James pg 38
4. Mantey pg 48

Chapter 7

1. Hill pg 51
2. Montgomery pg 58
3. Montgomery pg 60

Chapter 8

1. Define "fearfully" in hebrew pg 61

Chapter 9

1. Lindsey pg 70

Chapter 10

1. Nas, Original Gangsta pg 75
2. Montgomery pg 77
3. Anthony pg 77
4. Montgomery pg 77

Chapter 11

1. Define "Rejuvenate" pg 81
2. Lyles pg 81

Chapter 12

1. Cohen pg 89
2. Osei pg 92
3. Osei pg 93
4. Osei pg 94
5. Montgomery pg 94
6. Osei pg 94
7. Osei pg 95

Chapter 13

1. Day & Wiseman pg 99
2. Neighbors pg 100
3. Unknown pg 100
4. Unknown pg 100
5. Guzik pg 100
6. Guzik pg 101
7. Montgomery pg 102
8. Guzik pg 104
9. Montgomery pg 105
10. Jenkins 106
11. Osei 107

ABOUT THE AUTHOR

Ranae Kai is filled with God s peace and love. She is beyond excited to share His goodness with the world. Meeting and falling in love with our Heavenly Father was the absolute best thing that has ever happened to her.

She grew from loving the lifestyle she once knew to hating the lifestyle she once knew. Her desire for God compares to a buffet. She has an indescribable hunger that sincerely cares to sit at His feet and eat until overflow.

For Booking Contact:
441 747 4631

light@spiritofloveglobal.com
15201 Rockaway Blvd
#Z14144
Jamaica, NY 11434

www.ingramcontent.com/pod-product-compliance
Lightning Source LLC
Chambersburg PA
CBHW070401240426
43661CB00056B/2489